Proverbs
for
Programming
in
Pascal

Proverbs
for
Programming
in
Pascal

Louise E. Moser

California State University, Hayward

Andrew A. Turnbull

University of California, Berkeley

John Wiley & Sons
New York   Chichester   Brisbane   Toronto   Singapore

Library of Congress Cataloging-in-Publication Data

Moser, Louise E.
   Proverbs for Programming in Pascal.

   Bibliography: p.
   Includes index.
     1. PASCAL (Computer program language)
I. Turnbull, Andrew A.   II. Title.

QA76.73.P2M67 1985   005.13'3   85-16870
ISBN 0-471-82309-0

Printed in the United States of America

10 9 8 7 6 5 4 3 2 1

To the memory of my mother,

Agnes Hartlaub Moser

To the memory of my father,

Charles Herbert Turnbull

Preface

We were inspired to write *Proverbs for Programming in Pascal* because we wanted to help beginning and intermediate programming students to develop an effective programming style and have fun doing it! This book is intended for use either as an additional reference for students in programming, programming methods, and data structures courses or as a stand-alone text for students in programming methods courses who are already familiar with Pascal.

The 90 practical and inspirational proverbs contained within this text are designed to encourage the student to develop a high-quality style of programming. They address each phase of the software engineering process from the development of effective problem specifications and algorithms, to the programming of industrial strength solutions, to the preparation of useful documentation for the user as well as the maintenance programmer.

The main thrust of the proverbs is to emphasize the fundamental principles of structured programming and the elements of good programming style. Although we review some of the basics of auxiliary data storage, dynamic storage allocation, and recursion, this is not a book on the syntax of Pascal. Rather, our concern is with more subjective and conceptual issues of computer programming. The Pascal language was chosen only as as a vehicle for presenting these issues and principles.

We have organized the proverbs into 11 chapters, which include structuring one's time, structured programming methods, program legibility, robust programming, interactive programming, auxiliary data storage, recursion, dynamic storage allocation, program efficiency, testing and debugging, and documentation and maintenance. At the beginning of each chapter, we have included an introduction to motivate the particular topic and to introduce the proverbs in that chapter.

At the end of each chapter, we have included problems and projects of varying difficulty, which are designed to give the student an opportunity to apply the proverbs. We have provided more than enough for any one term; we don't expect anyone to complete all of the problems and projects in each chapter. Instructors who frequently have difficulty finding meaningful programming assignments should find Problems and Projects a welcome addition.

In this book we have included discussions of some concepts that are relatively new to the field of computer science, such as data abstraction, information hiding, and data flow diagrams. We have made reference to other disciplines, such as English, mathematics, statistics, and philosophy, to demonstrate their importance to computer science students. We have also included numerous examples and figures in the book to illustrate the proverbs and concepts being discussed.

The program fragments that make up most of the examples in this book are written in standard Pascal. Although they have been tested using Berkeley Pascal, this is, of course, no guarantee that they are correct (see Proverb 75). In fact, some of the examples that we have included are intentionally incorrect to demonstrate the particular point that we are trying to make; however, these examples are well marked. We would be grateful to hear of any errors (other than those intended) that you find in the program fragments or elsewhere in the text. We take great pride in our efforts, and any advice you have for improving the text would be greatly appreciated.

Students and instructors who use this book are encouraged to discuss the proverbs, helpful hints, and examples in class. We recognize that there may be differences of opinion on some of the suggestions and recommendations made in this book; however, this should serve as a springboard for discussion of these programming issues. Our aim in writing this book was simply to provide guidelines for writing well-structured, readable programs and to help students to develop quality programming skills and style. We hope that you find the book enlightening, entertaining, and inspirational!

About the Authors

As a professor-student team, the authors have approached this project from both sides of the academic picture. Dr. Louise Moser received her Ph.D. in Mathematics from the University of Wisconsin in 1970 and is currently a Professor of Mathematics and Computer Science at California State University, Hayward. Andrew Turnbull graduated in 1983 from CSU, Hayward, with a B.S. in Computer Science and received his M.B.A. from the University of California, Berkeley, in 1985.

Professor Moser has taught Programming Methods to hundreds of computer science students in Silicon Valley over the past several years. Having taught beginning programming courses in Fortran and Pascal and advanced courses in Data Structures, Analysis of Algorithms, and Operating Systems, she has an understanding of the difficulties that beginning students encounter and of the background needed by advanced students working in industry. She originally introduced programming proverbs as a special topic in her Programming Methods course. In this text she hopes to convey an appreciation of the logical and aesthetic philosophy behind structured programming.

Andrew Turnbull took an interest in learning about structured programming as a student in (and later as the reader for) Professor Moser's Programming Methods course. As an applications programmer for Sandia National Laboratories and as a product marketing engineer for Hewlett-Packard, he has had the opportunity to apply his academic training to his work and to exchange ideas with fellow programmers and software engineers. As a lab assistant at CSU, Hayward, and as a teaching assistant at UC, Berkeley, Mr. Turnbull has had first-hand experience assisting beginning programming students with their programming problems. His experiences at college and at work have influenced the emphasis of this book in applying programming proverbs to both academic and professional programming environments.

Acknowledgments

We wish to thank some very special people who played key roles in the production of this book. First and foremost, we wish to thank Michael Melliar-Smith for his expert technical advice and generous assistance. We would also like to give our appreciation to Betty Turnbull for her creative illustrations, to Karen Garner for her editing assistance and messenger service, and to Professor Moser's programming students for their helpful comments and criticisms of earlier versions of this text. Special thanks also go to our reviewers for their valuable advice. They are Professors William Dennison, Gary Ford, Lorraine Parker, Clifford Pelletier, Thomas C. Wesselkamper.

We wish to express our gratitude to the staff of John Wiley & Sons. In particular, we wish to thank Richard Bonacci, Martha Cooley, Gene Davenport, Laurie Ierardi, Ishaya Monokoff, and Elaine Rauschal. We also wish to thank Mary Forkner and David Fuchs for their assistance in the production of this book. We are pleased to be associated with John Wiley & Sons. In this, our first opportunity to work with Wiley, we found what we had heard is true: Wiley is a first-class organization.

Louise E. Moser

Andrew A. Turnbull

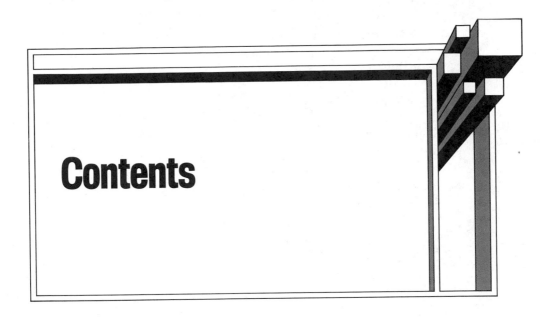

Contents

4   Robust Programming   102

5   Interactive Programming   133

6   Auxiliary Data Storage   150

Introduction

Welcome to a new academic term and a new programming course. As a programming student, you are in the process of developing programming habits that will influence your productivity and your success in a programming career. Soon you will be receiving programming assignments and a terminal connection to the computer!

In this text we have included 90 proverbs that are designed to offer you advice on structuring your time, structuring your programs, writing legible and robust programs, testing and debugging your programs, developing efficient programs, and maintaining and documenting your programs. Also included are proverbs that discuss auxiliary data storage, dynamic storage allocation, and recursion. Each proverb contains helpful hints and practical advice for making your programming efforts more productive.

The emphasis of this text is on the use of structured programming methods and good programming style. Structured programming methods are used by effective computer programmers in their work. These methods may be applied in each phase of software production—in developing problem specifications and algorithms, in writing the code for a program, in testing and debugging that code, and in documenting and maintaining the program over its lifetime.

Structured programs are written with clean logical design, descriptive identifiers, enlightening comments, and well-formatted layout. These

1

programs are written in a style that makes them easy to read, understand, debug, and maintain. Programming style is not "window dressing" that can be added after writing a program to make it look pretty, but it is embedded in the entire process of writing a program. Because the emphasis of this text is on subjective, conceptual issues of computer programming (rather than on the syntax of Pascal), you will want to use a Pascal textbook as a reference to supplement the discussions here.

Among the many features of this text are the numerous examples that illustrate how the proverbs may be applied in your projects. Some of the examples that we have included are intentionally wrong to demonstrate the particular point we are trying to make. These are marked by the logo

```
This is right.
Thus, it must be wrong.
```

with shading of the particular piece of code that is wrong. This logo will remind you that writing such fragments is something to be avoided.

By applying the proverbs offered you in this book, you will be well on your way to becoming an effective programmer. Don't hesitate to discuss any proverbs that you have questions about with your instructor. Also, watch how these proverbs are applied in your Pascal textbook, as well as in the examples here. As you are reading through this book, try to relate the proverbs to your own programming projects, and remember the proverb

> Nothing ever becomes real
>   till it is experienced.
> Even a proverb is no proverb to you
>   till your life has illustrated it.
>
>   —John Keats

1
Structuring Your Time

In this first chapter, we present some proverbs to help you make optimum use of your programming time. These proverbs provide advice for effectively scheduling your academic time, planning your programming efforts, developing problem definitions and solutions, and making use of computing resources.

As a computing student, you will experience the trials and tribulations of trying to get programming assignments completed without sacrificing other classes or (most important to any college student) leisure time. There are many hurdles over which you, as a computing student, will have to jump: The assignments are difficult, the instructor never gives you much time to finish the assigned programs, the computer center is crowded, and the computer can go down at any time. To top it all off, you still have to keep up with your other class assignments. These proverbs are designed to help you meet such challenges.

Of course, once you've made it through all of these hurdles, you may become a computing professional who is very much in demand. Computing professionals are of increasing importance to all types of businesses, and a firm's key to success may very well depend on the competent computer professionals it employs. Your employer will appreciate your knowing how to structure your computing efforts efficiently and, therefore, how to make the most of your time.

1 Keep time in its place.

The way in which you schedule your academic time will influence both your success and your attitude as a computing student. This first proverb is designed to encourage you to think carefully about how you choose your academic load. As you proceed through your college education, you can make your academic career more efficient and more satisfying by carefully choosing a balanced mix of classes in which to enroll. To provide variety in your schedule, we suggest that you enroll in nonquantitative "general education" courses during quarters or semesters when you take computer science courses.

You will soon find out that computer science courses often require long hours at the computer terminal. Unless you want to become "permanently attached" to the terminal, it's best to avoid taking too many computing courses at once. A student needs time away from computing homework, and some of this time can be used to work on assignments in other subjects, such as English or math.

In your professional career, you will find it a real asset to be able to write (and speak) in good, clear, simple English. Many more people will read the documents, proposals, and memos you will write than will read the code of your computer programs; therefore, you should put forth the effort to learn the art of expository writing. You will find that a strong background in mathematics is also important. Needless to say, many computer applications are highly quantitative in nature. Plan your course load carefully and organize your time so that you can be effective in both your computing courses and your general education courses.

If you are a beginning computing student, you must learn a great deal in your first classes. Beginners must learn the procedures for logging into and using the computer, the rules of a programming language, methods for solving programming problems, and the ways in which a programmer thinks. Thinking and planning are requirements for effective time management. Both on the job and at school (when you're taking several other classes), effective time management is a necessity.

During the time that you take your computing courses, you will not only need to allocate time for reviewing your class notes and for reading the text, but you will also need to make time for completing your programming assignments. Allow yourself enough time for each of the phases of program development: designing, coding, testing and debugging. Take time to plan your programs before you begin writing the code and typing it in at the terminal, and allow yourself enough time for debugging your programs and ensuring that they do the tasks for which they were designed.

You should plan to spend more homework time on your computing courses than on most of your other college courses. It is best if you schedule your daily affairs carefully and provide for plenty of time out of class to do your programming assignments.

2 Think first, second, and third; code later.

Before you begin writing code (and long before you even consider logging into the computer), it is very important to have your programming task clearly in mind and to develop a well-organized outline of your solution. In other words, **relax and think** about your project.

Many beginning programmers believe that they aren't accomplishing anything until they start poking away at the terminal keys and putting code into the computer. On the contrary, you don't need a pencil or terminal to begin the programming process. To begin working on your program, reread the programming assignment and make sure that you have no unanswered questions about the task at hand before you begin coding. Then, go on with your daily life as usual: Attend gym class, read your history assignments, or take a nap before you start coding. Often, the greatest breakthroughs in figuring out a solution to a problem come when you are relaxing or studying non-numeric or nonscientific subjects. The subconscious mind searches for answers even during sleep or recreation. Have you ever gone to bed at night with an unsolved problem and then awakened the next day with a solution? Let your subconscious do some of the work for you.

One undergraduate computer science student described his first project in his first programming job. He was assigned to a programming team with another novice programmer. The two young programmers were given a programming task that would take an entire summer. As beginners in this large-scale programming business, they wanted to get right to work coding their Fortran programs. After all, that was what they were used to doing at school! Fortunately, their supervisors were quick to tell them to put away their coding forms and spend at least a few days thinking about and planning their project. The student programmer commented, "Without thinking first and coding later, we never would have met our summer deadline."

Remember Murphy's Law of Programming:

> The sooner you start coding your program,
> the longer it is going to take.

3 Make the algorithm do the work.

The obvious first step in writing a program to solve a problem is to determine exactly what the problem is. When you have been asked to write a program, make sure that you have a clear understanding of the problem before proceeding. If the problem was given to you by someone else, make sure that you are interpreting the problem correctly. Some instructors, either intentionally or inadvertently, may give you a statement of a problem that is somewhat vague. Discuss any questions that you have about the problem with your instructor or the individual who assigned the problem to you.

A good understanding of the problem is essential to the construction of a good program. An incomplete understanding of the problem leads to wrong answers, omission of special cases, and even to unnecessary calculations. Time and thought are involved in understanding a problem. Hard work is required, but the pay-off comes when you run your program and it does what you intended it to do.

Understanding a problem involves three aspects.

1. Understanding what the objective is.

2. Understanding where the data are to come from and how they are laid out or formatted, and also what results are required and how they are to be formatted.

3. Understanding what processing is to be performed.

In your initial assignments, you will find yourself concentrating on the third aspect. But as you become more skilled and move on to more difficult assignments, you will find that it is the first and second aspects of understanding the problem that require the most attention (we will discuss these aspects in Proverb 4).

When you are thinking about the processing that will be needed, two aspects are important.

1. The data structures.[1]

2. The algorithm.[2]

Again, for more demanding assignments, it is the first of these, the data structures used for storing the data, that will require the most attention (we will discuss this further in Proverbs 11 to 13). But, initially, it is the concept of the algorithm that presents the greatest difficulty.

---

[1] Data structures—particular ways of organizing or arranging data for use by a computer.

[2] The word algorithm derives from the name of the author of a famous Arabic textbook on arithmetic (c. 825 A.D.). Abu Ja'far Mohammed ibu Mûsâ al-Khowârizmî took his name from the city of Khowârizm, now Chiva, near Samarkand in the USSR. The word algebra is derived from the title of this same textbook.

An algorithm is a statement of a method for solving a problem. To be useful in the development of a computer program, an algorithm should be

- Precise and unambiguous.

- A sequence of individual steps.

- Definite and effective.

- Finite.

The need for an algorithm to be precise and unambiguous sounds obvious. But there are few other activities in everyday life that require the kind of absolute precision and complete unambiguity needed for computer programming. Even with great care, things that appear obvious to you will be far from clear to others. Although it is possible to be precise in a natural language such as English, it is very difficult. Compare, for instance, the two statements "The men are tall and thin" and "The men are French and German." The meaning of the word "and" is quite different, indeed, almost exactly the opposite in meaning in the two cases. Therefore, instead of being expressed in English, algorithms are usually expressed in the formal and artificial languages of mathematics and of computer programming, such as Pascal.

When we describe an algorithm, we describe it as a sequence of small individual steps. Each of the steps must be completed before we start on the next step. Moreover, the algorithm must define the order in which the individual steps are to be performed. If a step is to be repeated, then it must define when to stop the repetition. In everyday life, we are often not very careful in defining the order of steps, and sometimes things go wrong as a result. For example, we would say, "Put on your shoes and socks," really meaning socks first. Unfortunately, the computer will follow your instructions blindly.

Requiring an algorithm to be definite implies that it must be clear exactly what operation is to be performed at each step, and it must be clear exactly what data the operation is to be performed on. Just as the algorithm itself has input (the initial data) and output (the results), so each step of the algorithm has input (the operands) and output (the result). One of the most common errors in the design of an algorithm is the use of an undefined data value as input to one of the steps. For instance, it is easy to declare a variable tota l and use it to sum a sequence of values without first setting tota l to zero.

If the algorithm contains conditional steps in which one of two alternative steps is performed, the condition that selects which alternative is chosen must be definitely true or definitely false when the choice is made. Even if it does not matter which choice is made, we must still make a definite choice if we are to convert the algorithm into a programming language like Pascal.

The concept of effective is more subtle. It requires that each step of the algorithm process only information that is available at the time of that step. Instructions such as "Turn left at the second street before the post office" are not effective because it is not possible to know that the street is the one required until one reaches the post office and is far beyond the second street. A similar example is the "optimal" space allocation algorithm for computers. This algorithm removes from storage the information that will not be needed for the longest time into the future. In general, algorithms such as these are not effective because the program cannot anticipate the future.

The requirement for finiteness refers less to the finite size of the description of the algorithm than to the ability to complete the algorithm by executing a finite number of individual steps. A program that computes forever without returning any results is of little use (we will discuss this in Proverb 80). Indeed, we require that the algorithm be completed in as few steps as possible, so as to obtain good performance. The computational cost of an algorithm is an important topic in computer science and is discussed in Proverb 69.

Let's now review the necessary attributes of an algorithm by considering a (not so) futuristic example. Suppose that you have won a very lucrative scholarship from Roger Wilco Robotics, Inc., and that as part of this scholarship you have been given a robot to help you with your domestic chores. Desiring an extra hour of leisure, you decide to have your new robot do the laundry for you. Because the android responds to commands in simple English and can remember a sequence of commands, all you have to do is provide it with an algorithm for laundering

your clothes. After showing the robot where the washing machine, the soap, and your dirty laundry are located, you tell the robot

> Open the lid and
>   put the clothes into the machine.
> Put in some laundry detergent and
>   start the machine.
> When the buzzer goes off,
>   put the clothes in the dryer.

As we can see, this algorithm is a sequence of individual steps. Unfortunately, it is neither precise nor unambiguous. One reason is that the necessary amount of laundry detergent is not sufficiently defined. "Some" to the robot could mean a teaspoonful or the entire box. Furthermore, an important step was omitted—close the lid!

After cleaning up all of the soapy water that spilled out on the laundry room floor, you decide to teach the robot how to dry the clothes. So you give him the following instructions:

Once you have put all the clothes in the dryer,
    shut the lid and
    start the dryer.
If the buzzer goes off,
    open the lid and
    see if the clothes are dry.
If they are not,
    close the lid and
    run the machine for 5 more minutes.
Each time the buzzer goes off,
    follow my two previous instructions
    until the clothes become dry.
When the clothes are dry,
    put them in the basket and
    bring them to me.

This algorithm contains some conditional steps, for example, "If the buzzer goes off." It also contains steps that are to be repeated and provides the conditions under which those steps are to be repeated. In particular, if the buzzer goes off and the clothes are not dry, the robot is to continue running the machine for 5 extra minutes.

Because you have specified what to do when the clothes are dry and when they are not dry, the algorithm is definite. It is also effective because you only asked the robot to process information that is available at the time of each step. Finally, assuming the dryer is working properly, the clothes will eventually become dry, and therefore the algorithm is finite.

Although the Pascal programs that you write are indeed algorithms, it's best to think of an algorithm as a general method of solving a problem, rather than as a specific method particular to just one program. General-purpose algorithms are powerful techniques that can be applied to many different programs time and time again. Once a general algorithm has been chosen and appropriate data structures are designed, you understand enough about the method of solving the problem that it's easy to refine the algorithm into an efficient Pascal program. By developing a repertoire of general-purpose algorithms, you will make programming easier for yourself, and in the long run you will save yourself a lot of time.

4 It's hard to see how to proceed without specs.

When the request for a program has originated with someone else, it's a good idea for you, the programmer, and the problem originator to work together in preparing a definition of the program and in formulating its specifications. The originator of the request may have overlooked aspects of the problem or may not have an appreciation of the capabilities and limitations of the particular computer. But he or she usually will have a good understanding of what is needed and why. A discussion with the originator may clarify the problem for both of you.

Take time to prepare a concise, but precise, written definition of what is to be done. Both you and the person requesting your programming services should agree on what is to be done before you proceed to develop detailed specifications. Such a problem statement may be no more than a sentence or two, or it may be several paragraphs. The detail of the statement depends on the complexity of the program and the familiarity of the programmer with the task to be done.

In formulating specifications for a program, start by determining what output you want the program to produce. Also, consider the form the output should take. Is the objective to produce a report like a financial statement, a file such as mailing addresses in zip code order, or simply the result of a calculation with a few informative labels? The answer to this question will affect how you design your program solution. Before going any further, you should come to an agreement with the problem originator as to what output is required and how it should look.

Once you have determined the output to be produced, look at the input that you are given. Consider the form in which this input is given. Will it be typed in by the user at a terminal, or is the input to be read in from a file on a disk? What does each data item in the input represent? Does the input consist of integers, real numbers, or characters? For introductory problems, the answers to these questions might seem trivial; however, advanced applications may entail reading from several different input files and accepting many different input values. It is important to have a thorough understanding of the input with which you will be working.

Because the purpose of your program is to produce the desired output from the given input, the next part of the specification should include a high-level description of what is to be done with the input data to produce the output result. This description does not have to be excessively detailed, and it need not provide a detailed algorithm or solution design. But it should include formulas for calculations and any other special information the programmer needs to design the algorithm. Again, be sure to consult with the problem originator to ensure that your description of what is to be done corresponds to his or her expectations.

Let's consider a simple example. Suppose that Movin' Manny wants a program to determine how far he can run at a given rate and in a given amount of time. He wants the program to prompt him for a rate and a time and then, after he has entered these numbers into the terminal, to print the distance traveled. As Manny's programmer, you begin by discussing the problem with him and by writing the following problem definition:

> The program will prompt the user for a rate and a
> time, calculate the distance traveled, and then output
> this result to the terminal.

After you have written the problem definition, you then determine the output that is required. Insofar as the distance should be a real number between 0 and 100, Manny wants the output to look like this:

The distance traveled is *xxx.xx* miles.

Having dealt with the output, you now look carefully at what the input will be.

> From the terminal you will read in a rate in miles per hour and a time in minutes. Both the rate and the time will be real numbers.

Finally, you write a description of what is to be done with the input to produce the desired output.

> Prompt the user and accept the input.

> Convert the time from minutes to hours, using the following formula:

$$\text{time in hours} = \text{time in minutes}/60$$

> Calculate the distance, using the following formula:

$$\text{distance} = \text{rate} \times \text{time}$$

> Output the result to the terminal.

With these detailed specifications, you are ready to design an algorithm (in this rather simple case, there is not much more to do) and write the code for the solution.

As you work on more advanced applications, you will find that the simple aspects of a program are easy to specify but are also easy to program correctly. As you gain experience in designing programming solutions, you'll spend time concentrating on the more difficult parts of the problem.

We now give a real-life example that illustrates what not to do. A programmer who was to write the scheduling program for a steel mill's hot strip mill was very worried about how to design the scheduling algorithm. The problem was difficult and depended on the needs of the customers, the type of steel, the scratching of the mill's rollers, and many other factors. But the operations research people said that there was no problem; they had researched it and produced a specification of what was required in the form of a flowchart.

The programmer dived in and waded through excruciatingly detailed instructions on how to read the data, how to sort the data into this order and that order, and how to organize the data into tables, until he reached a box containing the instruction, without any other form of explanation, "Choose most appropriate strip to roll." The operations research people had specified everything that he didn't need to be told and had omitted the only information that he really needed.

There is no easy rule as to what constitutes a good specification; the circumstances determine what is appropriate. If you are describing a problem to a highly skilled programmer who is familiar with your system, a very terse specification will suffice. On the other hand, if you are writing a specification for an inexperienced programmer or for the programmer who is not familiar with your system, you will have to provide much more information. Indeed, when you, as a highly skilled programmer, receive an outline specification, you will start to assemble all of this information for your own use and as a part of the program documentation.

In developing a specification, here is some information that you will need to know. This list is by no means exhaustive, but it provides a guideline that will help you in writing a good specification.

- You will need to know what output is required and how it is to be presented. This will depend, for example, on whether you are producing reports for other people to read or creating files for use by other programs.

- You will need to identify the input, including both interactive input from the terminal and input from files. You will need to know what the format of this data should be and what each data item represents.

- You will need to understand the procedural rules of the organization and how these rules will affect the program. For example, a programmer for a brokerage house not only needs to know about rules such as

  > Options do not count as sales when they are granted;
  > they become sales only when they are exercised.

  but also what such a rule means as far as coding the program is concerned. Understanding such rules is accomplished by working closely with the problem originator to develop the specifications.

- You will need to decide how, and by whom, the program is going to be run. There are very great differences between a batch program to be run overnight by a professional operator and an interactive program to serve a user who is not very familiar with computers. Consider the contrast, for instance, between these two error messages:

  > Extent overflow on monthly sales file.
  > Assign new file extent.

  and

  > Shipping date missing.
  > Input target shipping date.

- Knowing who is to use the program, you must note what standards have been established for interaction with that type of user. These standards will be very different for professional computer staff as compared with users whose professional interests lie elsewhere. Such standards really are very important because they establish uniformity. Computer systems in which every program has its own private conventions for error correction, strings across line boundaries, etc., are very aggravating to the user.

- You will need to make decisions relating to resources (e.g., no graphics because of time constraints) and strategy (e.g., recompute the data every time a sales manager runs the program instead of precomputing and storing the data in a file).

There are really no simple divisions between requirements, specifications, design, and documentation. They represent a continuous sequence of increasingly more detailed descriptions of the program. At every level, understanding the problem, clarity of expression, and attention to the issues of importance are what matter.

5 Write it out before you type it in.

After you have relaxed, thought about your problem, and developed an algorithm and specifications for your program, prepare in detail what you will type into the terminal. Write your program, complete with comments, on paper from which you can read when you are typing.

There are a number of benefits from having your code ready to type. First, you can do most of your programming work at your desk, in the library, or in your hot tub before entering the crowded computer lab. You will also spend less time at the terminals. (If everyone spent less time at the terminals, the computer labs wouldn't be so crowded, and those logged into the machine would enjoy faster response time.) Best of all, you can catch a lot of errors by writing your program in detail on sheets of paper where errors are more easily discovered.

As you write each small fragment, step through it with sample data to see if the code produces the correct output. Unless your program is very small, you probably won't want to step through the entire program in this way. But by stepping through each fragment, you can catch a lot of errors in your program before you type it into the terminal.

To save time and to make your work at the terminal easier, try to learn as much as you can about the editor for your system. An editor is itself a computer program, written for you by someone else, that facilitates the creation and modification of text. Most editors include commands for inserting lines, deleting lines, replacing one string by another, shifting fragments of code around in a program, etc. Ask your instructor or a computer lab assistant how you can get a hard copy[3] of the document that describes the available commands on the editor for your system.

---

[3]Hard copy—a listing on paper.

6 D' bugs will eat up your time.

After you have typed in your program, you can then compile it. (If you don't know how, ask your instructor or a lab assistant for the command for compiling a Pascal program on your system.) A compiler is a computer program that converts your code into a form that can be executed by the machine. It will also find the syntax errors in your program. Syntax errors occur when the rules of the language in which you have written your program are violated. Common syntax errors in Pascal include misplaced semicolons, missing **end**'s, and misspelled identifiers. Once these syntax errors are located, you can go ahead and correct them. You should be able to correct most syntax errors in your program quite quickly.

If, after you have corrected all of the syntax and typing errors, you find that your program is not doing what you want or expect it to do, then it has logic errors. Logic errors are sometimes signaled when, for example, the value of an array subscript or a case selector goes out of range. However, often logic errors are more difficult to detect. You will need to design a test plan, which includes selected test cases for which you will run your program to determine whether it still has logic errors.

If you find that the results from testing are not as you had expected, then your program probably has logic errors and needs debugging. Debugging can be the most time-consuming portion of a programming project; often, more time is spent in debugging a program than in writing it originally. (Chapter 10 of this book is dedicated entirely to testing and debugging a program.)

The most effective means of debugging is to trace[4] the values of the variables during the execution of your program. This can be done by using an interactive "debugger" or by putting "debugging write statements" in your program to print the values of the variables.

Such debugging write statements should be included in your program from the very beginning and should be left in your program for future debugging and maintenance. They can be included in conditional statements and turned on and off with a switch. Set up a boolean[5] variable, such as debugging, so that you can write

```
if debugging then
    writeln( ... );
```

When you're debugging your program, you can then turn on the switch by setting debugging equal to true. And voila, your write statements will give you all kinds of exciting information about the execution of your code!

Alternatively, you can use an interactive debugger, if such a facility is available on your system. A debugger is a computer program that allows you to ask questions interactively about the execution of your program in order to find logic errors or to test the program code.

Remember, by looking at the values of the variables during the execution of your program, you can locate the errors much more easily than by just staring at the code. (You'll find a more complete discussion of this topic in Proverb 79.)

---

[4]Trace (when used as a noun)—a listing of the values of variables during execution of a program.

[5]Boolean—true or false. This derives from George Boole (1815-1864), who is well-known for his work in algebra and logic. Because boolean is a predefined identifier in Pascal, for consistency we write boolean in lower case throughout the text.

7 You'll find no bugs staring at the terminal.

When your program has logic errors, you will not solve the problem by staring at the terminal. The only way to solve the problem is by thinking about it, and this thinking is best done away from the terminal.

First, you will need to produce a trace of the values of your program variables and a full listing of your program. Then log off and go away from the terminal to a place where you can sit comfortably and think about why your program is not working as you intended and how those variables came to have the values that they now have. At the terminal, tension mounts as the time passes when you're having difficulty finding bugs, and "quick fixes" are likely to cause even more problems and more frustration. If you think about your problem at a desk or a table away from the terminal, you will find the logic errors in your program much more quickly.

Furthermore, in a university environment where there are many students waiting to use the terminals, it's a matter of common courtesy to do your thinking away from the terminal. While you're sitting at the terminal, thinking about your program, you are not using the computer, but you are tying up a terminal that could be used by someone else. Some university computer centers have placed time limits on the use of terminals to enable more students to use the machines.

8 Don't reinvent the wheel.

In most programming courses, each of the students in the class is usually asked to write a program to solve the same problem. Usually, these problems have been solved many times before by other programmers. In professional environments, however, it is inefficient for more than one person to do the same task. Professional programmers are advised to share their programs with their colleagues, so that no one is "reinventing the wheel" by duplicating someone else's effort.

To avoid duplication of effort, most companies encourage their programmers to use program libraries. Program libraries contain files of canned routines[6] that solve particular problems or perform particular tasks. These libraries may include mathematical routines, input/output routines, graphics packages, and statistical analysis programs. They may include routines for sorting, searching, solving systems of linear equations, finding the roots of a polynomial, or generating random numbers.

Although there may be little need for using library routines in your first few programming courses, you will find such routines very helpful when programming more advanced applications. By using canned library routines you can spend your time working on bigger and better things!

---

[6]Canned routines—programs and subprograms that are already written for you.

Certainly, in professional settings it makes sense to use library routines because they are already written and tested, and they are easy to use.

Although external library routines may be called from within a Pascal program, standard Pascal does not specify exactly how this is to be done. On one particular system, for example, to use an external routine that generates random numbers in a program, you must include the following "comment" after the program heading

```
(*$I'RANDOM' RANDOM NUMBER GENERATOR DECLARATIONS.*)
```

Once this is included, you can then call the random number generator in the program wherever you want to use it. But on another system, access to such an external routine may be quite different. Consult the lab assistants, systems programmers, and user manuals at your computer center to learn how to use the routines in your program library. However, be advised that programs contained in program libraries are often copyrighted. Although you can use these programs, you must not copy them or take them away.

Problems and Projects

1. Get a hard copy of the document that describes the available commands for the editor of your system. Experiment with and learn how to use these commands.

2. The IEEE (Institute for Electrical and Electronics Engineers) has established a specification outline (IEEE 830) that gives a good framework from which to write a specification. It appears, for example, in "Preventing Software Requirements Specification Errors with IEEE 830," edited by Robert M. Poston, *IEEE Software* (Vol. 2, No. 1), January 1985 (p. 85). Study the specification outline and discuss it in class.

3. Consider the following problem statement:

    > Given daily time cards, containing a worker's hourly wage and number of hours worked, compute his or her weekly take-home pay.

What information is missing or inadequate for the problem to be completely and unambiguously defined? Make some assumptions about the missing information and rewrite the specification.

4. Develop specifications for a program to calculate average scores of players of a sport, such as baseball players' batting averages. The specifications should include the input and output to the program and also the operations to be performed. For help, see Proverb 4.

5. You are planning a seven-course dinner and you need an algorithm to prepare a shopping list. Each ingredient is to be listed once, along with the quantity required for all of the dishes you are going to make. You may assume that the recipes, which come from your computerized cookbook, are all given in the same unit of measurement. The algorithm you develop should be only the first step toward a program at the same level of detail as the example in Proverb 3.

6. Many banks, money market companies, and savings and loan institutions compute interest on a daily basis. This means that if you start with a balance of, say, $1000 and the interest rate is, say, 9%, then the interest you will earn during the first day is $1000 \times 0.09/365$ (because it is for 1 day of a 365-day year). This yields 0.25 and a new balance of $1000.25. The interest you will earn during the second day is then $0.09 \times 1000.25/365$, etc. Design an algorithm that takes three inputs—the amount of a deposit, the interest rate (as a percent), and the number of years (which may be a fractional part of a year)—and that computes and prints the balance in the account at the end of this time period.

7. Most computer centers have among their canned routines a routine that generates random numbers. A random number is a number that has the same probability of being chosen as any other number in the range of possible values. If your computer center has such a "random number generator," use it to generate seven-letter computer passwords. Hint: Set up an array

```
var
    password: array[1..7] of char;
```

and generate the letters of the password, one at a time, by calling the random number generator seven times. If, for example, the letters of the alphabet correspond to the integers 1 to 26 on your computer, `chr(n)` will give you the letter corresponding to the integer n between 1 and 26. If the call to the random number generator is `rand(x)` on your computer, and `rand(x)` returns a real number x such that $0 \leq x < 1$, then `trunc(26 * rand(x) + 1)` will give you a random integer n such that $1 \leq n \leq 26$.

2
Structured
Programming

Structured programming methods are the basis for developing pro
grams that are understandable and correct. In this chapter we will present
proverbs for effective structured programming. We will discuss structured
design tools, data abstraction, modularization, and methods for improving the logical structure of your programs.

Here, you'll read about the historic "structure theorem" and the
famous "**goto** controversy." You'll see how we apply structured design
methods to the very highbrow academic and culinary pursuit of baking a
cake. You'll read about (soon to become) famous firms, such as Willy
Liker's Fly-by-Night Computer Dating Service and Phyllis's Physical
Fitness Farm, and how they find solutions to business problems using
structured programming techniques. As you'll soon learn, it pays to become an expert at applying the proverbs for structured programming.

9 Top down and bottom up
are the ladder to all high designs.

The best approach to solving a new problem is the method of top-
down design, also referred to as the method of successive, or stepwise,
refinement. In this approach to problem solving we divide our problems

up into subproblems, divide subproblems into still smaller subproblems, and continue in this way until we have very small subproblems that can be solved easily.

For example, Galactic Business Machines, Inc., has asked us to write a program to process orders for computers. Assuming that we have completed a set of specifications as prescribed in Proverb 4, we are ready to design an algorithm for the program. To begin our stepwise refinement, we state the problem:

> Process order

But immediately we break this into subproblems:

> Read in order
> Check client's credit
> For each item in order:
>   Check item in stock
>   Update stock file
> Back-order out of stock items
> Print shipping order
> Print bill
> Debit client's account

Next, we subdivide each of these into further subproblems. For example, "Back-order out of stock items" might become

> For each item that is out of stock:
>   Check existing back order and
>   minimum quantity that can be ordered
>   Choose supplier with best price for item
>   Print order for item
>   Update order file

When we are subdividing our subproblems further, we do not look at each individually. Rather, we select some aspect of the problem and identify all of the subproblems that are related to it. For instance, in the example above, we should consider the subproblems "Read in order," "For each item in order," and "Print shipping order" together, because they all involve the client's order. The aspect of the problem that requires our attention is the client's order, and as a result of our decision about how we handle the client's order, each of the three subproblems will be divided up in ways that are compatible. We try to make these three subdivisions in a way that concerns only the aspect that we are concentrating on, namely the client's order.

Top-down design will almost certainly enable you to solve your problem, but the resulting program may not be very efficient. There is a risk that the same processing may be done repeatedly in each of several subproblems. At each stage of your design work, you must consider whether the program you are designing will result in such duplicated processing. You must also be willing to modify your design into a logically equivalent design that is solved more efficiently.

We can also use bottom-up design, not as an alternative to topdown design but, rather, in conjunction with it. Whereas top-down design begins with the problem and works down toward the machine, bottom-up design starts with the machine and works up toward the application. Clearly, we can use both techniques together to meet in the middle.

In bottom-up design, we begin with the basic data types and operations of the machine. At the lowest levels, we have binary numbers and the basic operations defined on them. On top of these are built integers and real numbers with the operations of addition, subtraction, multiplication, and division. But these are still really rather too simple to be ideal for our applications, and thus for each application we devise some data structures of our own and also our own operations, programmed as procedures and functions. Next we use these data structures and operations to define more complex data structures and operations that are even more suited to our particular application. Our objective is to produce data structures and operations so appropriate to our needs that programming the particular problem becomes very easy. In effect, we are trying to build a "virtual machine" that is custom designed for our use.

Bottom-up design leads to the notion of abstract data types, which we will discuss in Proverb 11. The design of modern programming languages has been influenced strongly by bottom-up design. Many of the most recent languages, particularly the Ada language, have been designed by extending Pascal to include more comprehensive features for abstract data types to support bottom-up design. The strategy of bottom-up design, as the term was used a few years ago, is the same as that described here. But now we are more skillful at using bottom-up design because we have a better understanding of abstract data types.

Bottom-up design is particularly effective for producing compact and efficient programs. It is also very appropriate if you must produce many programs in the same application area, programs that can all use the same set of abstract data types. But bottom-up design requires a thorough understanding of the particular problem you're trying to solve. If you start on bottom-up design too soon before you really understand the overall design of your program, the data structures and operations you design may turn out to be quite unsuited to your actual needs.

10 Power up with programming tools.

We now offer some structured design tools that will help you to develop your algorithms and prepare for the actual coding of your programs in Pascal. One structured programming tool that promotes top-down design of an algorithm is the structure chart. The structure chart is a graphic representation of the hierarchy of program tasks. It presents a programming task from the general to the particular, with emphasis on what must be done rather than how it must be done.

Because structure charts are tools of logic, they can be used to outline algorithms for doing nonprogramming, as well as programming, tasks. As an example of how to prepare and use a structure chart, let's look at a task that is not yet (we believe) being accomplished by a computer—making a cake (Fig. 2.1).

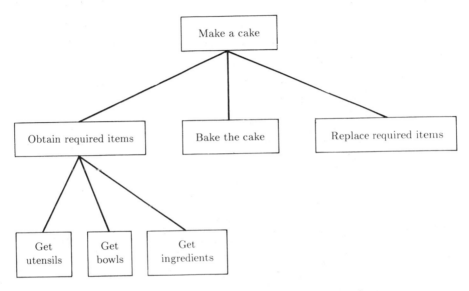

Figure 2.1 Structure chart for making a cake.

In this "high-tech" method of making a cake, note that

1. The purpose of the main module,[1] which is represented by the uppermost box and is sometimes called the driver,[2] is to direct the modules below it, which are executed in order from left to right.

2. If a module is subdivided further, then the module's purpose is to direct all of the modules below it, which are executed from left to right. For example, the module labeled "Obtain required items"

---

[1]Module—a logical part of a design or program, such as a procedure or function.

[2]Driver—a program written for the express purpose of calling certain procedures and functions.

will direct the three modules below it, which further define, in detail, the tasks of obtaining the required items: "Get utensils," "Get bowls," and "Get ingredients."

3. Each module has one entry and one exit point.

4. The cake maker executes the modules in the following manner.

   (a) The main module transfers control to the left-most module below it. In this case, "Make a cake" transfers control to "Obtain required items."

   (b) The "Obtain required items" module completes all of its tasks or instructions (which include all of the modules below it) and then transfers control back to the main module.

   (c) The main module then transfers control to the "Bake the cake" module. This module calls on all of the modules below it (which might include "Place in oven," "Set alarm," etc.) and then transfers control back to the main module.

   (d) The main module transfers control to the module "Replace required items." This module directs control to the modules below it (which entail the highly complicated processes of putting the required items away). As each of these modules completes its task, control returns to the "Replace required items" module. After the module has directed all of the replacements, control is returned to the main module, which terminates the process of making a cake.

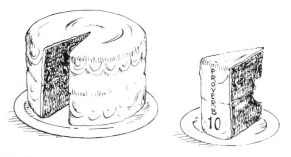

THIS PROVERB IS A PIECE OF CAKE!

During the early stages of planning and development, the structure chart can be an effective tool for determining the overall organization of your program. The structure chart is most effective in describing the high-level structure of your program. Trying to continue the same chart down to too much detail, however, produces a "rat's nest," which is very hard to understand.

Once the overall plan is in place, you can proceed from the general plan to coding the particular modules outlined in the chart. At that stage, think of each module below the main module as a procedure or function and the main module as the main program, which does nothing more than call on its subordinate procedures and functions to perform their tasks. (For more on this, don't miss Proverbs 18 and 19.)

Although structure charts are effective tools for high-level planning, you will eventually reach the portions of your task that require conditional branching and iteration. In the past you might have used a flowchart or control flow diagram (Fig. 2.3) as a graphic tool to describe the flow of control of a program, that is, the sequence of operations that are executed from the start of the program to the end.

The flowchart was used for many years by people planning their computer algorithms, but in recent years, flowcharts have fallen out of favor because most programmers find Pascal programs just as easy to read and write as flowcharts and also because, compared with a Pascal program, flowcharts are more difficult to store in a computer, to edit, to update, and to print out. Nevertheless, they are still used in many technical and business applications in industry and government.

Another graphic tool that you might find useful is the data flow diagram or bubble chart (Fig. 2.4). As its name suggests, such a diagram describes the flow of data through a program, that is, the dependencies of the data input to, and calculated by, the program. A data flow diagram consists of a circle or bubble for each item of data that is input or calculated. The arrows indicate what subsequent calculation the data is used for and under what conditions it might be used.

The data flow diagram is more useful than the flowchart because it is more difficult to trace the flow of data than the flow of control by casual inspection of program code. Using a data flow diagram, you can readily determine all of the subsequent uses of each item of data and, also, how each item of data came to be a certain value, that is, what values went into forming the value you have for that data item. It is much easier to determine the value of an item of data from a data flow diagram than from conventional programming diagrams or code, where the information is often spread throughout the entire program.

Data flow diagrams are used extensively in program documentation. Insofar as you will probably have to produce a data flow diagram for your program sooner or later, you might as well begin with it and have it available to help you write your program.

To illustrate the use of flowcharts and data flow diagrams, we now consider a method of finding a solution to the equation $f(x) = 0$. The method, called the interval bisection method, is usually studied in calculus, but the idea is really very simple. The solution to the equation is approximated by successively dividing the interval $[a, b]$ into two, until a solution is found with a desired degree of accuracy, which we call ϵ.[3] The method applies when a function f is continuous on an interval $[a, b]$ and has opposite signs at its endpoints—as, for example, shown in Fig. 2.2.

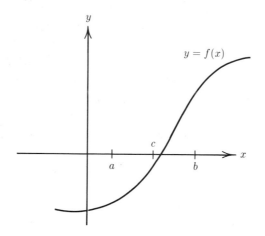

Figure 2.2 Interval bisection method.

In developing a program for the interval bisection method, we produce a flowchart and data flow diagram, as shown in Figs. 2.3 and 2.4.

---

[3]This is the Greek letter epsilon. It is often used to represent a very small positive number, usually the tolerable error in a calculation.

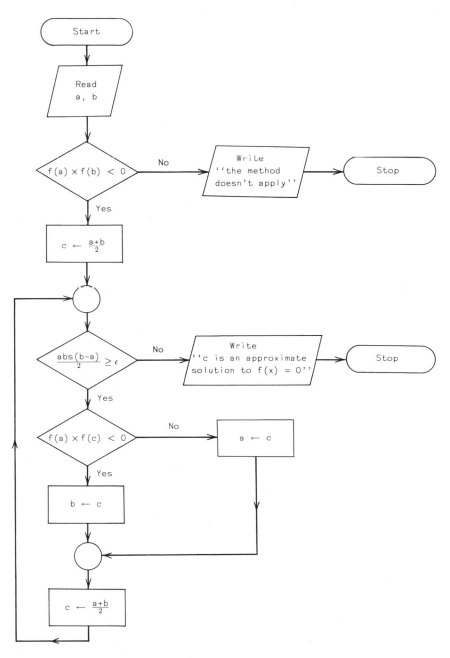

Figure 2.3 Flowchart for the interval bisection method.

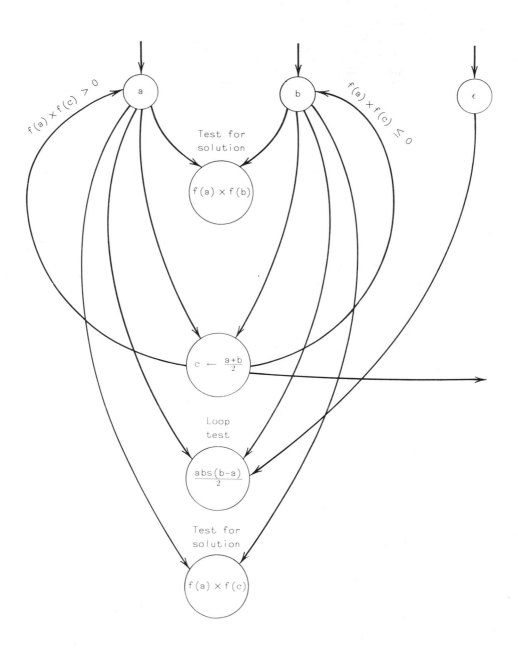

Figure 2.4 Data flow diagram for the interval bisection method.

Structure charts and data flow diagrams are useful tools for uncovering the two-dimensional nature of an algorithm and providing a "blueprint" of it. For many programmers and software engineers, they serve as a "universal language" that facilitates the translation of ideas into one of many programming languages. You may find that a nonprogrammer, with whom you may be working on a computing project, will have an easier time understanding the logic of your program when it is demonstrated graphically than when it is written into code. Structure charts and data flow diagrams can serve as useful tools for a person who later needs to understand how your program works. Therefore, don't throw away these diagrams when you get your program to run; instead, include them in the documentation for your program. (We'll talk more about documentation in Proverb 88.)

Once you have developed the blueprint for your program, the next step in the method of top-down planning involves the use of "pseudocode." Pseudocode is an English-like program documentation language that closely resembles Pascal but doesn't require the syntactical precision that the Pascal compiler requires. Your instructor (and eventually your employer) may emphasize some particular guidelines for writing pseudocode, but for your own needs you may develop your own pseudocoding style. Here is an example in which a programmer uses pseudocode to outline tasks to be accomplished during a given week:

```
case day of

    sun: take a rest;

    mon: generate last week's data summary;

    tue: update data file;

    wed: process new data;

    thu: generate statistics;

    fri: generate report;

    sat: goof off

end;
```

As the programmer later moves to the next level of program development, he or she fills in the details of the various tasks to be accomplished each day. Once the pseudocode becomes sufficiently detailed, the programmer can handcheck the algorithm and then type the Pascal statements into the computer terminal.

Here is another example. It demonstrates how you might translate the flowchart and data flow diagram in Figs. 2.3 and 2.4 into Pascal-like pseudocode.

```
read in a,b

if f(a),f(b) opposite signs then (* There's a solution
                                     in the interval
                                     with endpoints a,b *)

   c ← (a + b)/2              (* (a+b)/2 is the midpoint
                                 of the interval *)

   while not yet accurate enough do

     if f(a),f(c) opposite signs then (* There's a solution
                                          in the interval
       b ← c                           with endpoints a,c *)

     else                         (* There's a solution
                                      in the interval
       a ← c                      with endpoints b,c *)

     c ← (a + b)/2

   write 'c is an approximate solution
          to the equation f(x) = 0'

else

   write 'the method doesn't apply'
```

Many programmers skip over the structure chart and data flow diagram and proceed directly to pseudocode, particularly for simple programs. But pseudocode is not really a structured technique, and it's just as easy to produce an unstructured program as a structured one with pseudocode.

Just as a modern programming language supports you in bottom-up design, structured programming tools, such as the structure chart and the data flow diagram, aid you in designing your programs in a top-down fashion. Remember, the main goal of top-down structured design is to aid you in developing well-structured modular programs that are easier to design, easier to write, easier to debug, easier to document and explain to somebody else and, in particular, easier for you to understand and thus more likely to be correct. The bottom line is that time spent up front on structured design saves you more time in the end.

11 Elegant design hides the mechanism.

One of the best methods for structuring your program is the technique of data abstraction, also referred to as the use of abstract data types. This technique, perhaps the most effective structuring technique known, requires both a lot of practice and a deep understanding of the problem at hand. As you become more skilled in programming, you will find that this proverb is one of the most valuable to you.

In the method of data abstraction, we try to think of ideal data structures, data structures that are more complex than the basic data types (integer, real, char, and boolean) and that, once they are provided, greatly simplify the task of programming a problem. We choose not only the data structure but also the operations that are to be used to manipulate it, operations that we will program as procedures and functions. Our objective is that the data structure should be manipulated only by these operations and that there should be no other direct manipulation of it. We can then write our program using the abstract data type and the operations defined on it in just the same way that we use a built-in type, like the type real with the operations of addition, subtraction, multiplication, and division defined on it.

An example of a high-level abstract data type might be an appointments calendar. We do not need to say exactly what the data structure representing the calendar is (it might be an array or a linked list[4]), but we assume the declaration of a calendar data type.

```
type
    calendar = ...
```

Then, we must define a constant, an empty calendar, and a suitable set of operations on the calendar, such as

Insertappointment	takes a calendar, a date, a time, and a name and records the appointment.
Deleteappointment	takes a calendar, a date, a time, and a name and deletes the appointment.
Nextappointment	takes a calendar, a date, and a time and returns the name, date, and time of the next appointment.
Availabletimes	takes a calendar and a date and returns a list of available times.
Nextvisitof	takes a calendar and a name and returns the next appointment for that name.

These operations enable us to perform manipulations of calendars, and the rest of the program should use them in preference to direct manipulation of the calendar data structure itself. Part of the reason for this is to keep our programs as high level as possible, and part of the reason is to ensure that our programs do not depend on the particular choice of representation for the abstract data type. For example, if we decide to change the representation of a calendar from an array to a linked list, only the five procedures above will require modification, and the rest of the program can remain unchanged.

---

[4]Linked list—a way of organizing data. We will talk about linked lists in Chapter 8.

We can think of an abstract data type as a black box.[5] The data structure is hidden inside the black box, and the operations are the knobs and levers by which the data structure is manipulated. One advantage of this black box, or "information hiding," approach is that the programs that use the abstract data type do not depend on the specific nature of the data structure. Thus, we can change the details of that structure, perhaps to gain efficiency, without upsetting the rest of the program. But the most important advantage of data abstraction is seen when a master programmer is able to define a very simple set of operations with all the complexity hidden inside the black box. This can greatly simplify the rest of the program and make it much easier to understand.

12 Simple is the sign of skill.

In his 1980 Turing award lecture, "The Emperor's Old Clothes," C.A.R. Hoare stated

> There are two ways of constructing a software design:
> One way is to make it so simple that there are obvi-
> ously no deficiencies, and the other way is to make it
> so complicated that there are no obvious deficiencies.
> The first method is far more difficult.[6]

When you're designing your programs, strive for simplicity. It is particularly important to choose the simplest data structures that are appropriate for the data you are trying to represent. You can build very complex structures in Pascal, but complex data structures require

---

[5]Black box—people who make electronics products often make black boxes that do some particular task. Once the black box is made, you don't have to worry about how it is made; you only need to know what it does and how to use it.

[6]C.A.R. Hoare, "The emperor's old clothes." *Communications of the ACM*, 24:2 (1981), p. 81. Reprinted with the permission of the Association of Computing Machinery.

complex programs to manipulate them. Try to choose data structures
that make a program simple by providing direct access to the most important items in the data.

For example, if you were a programmer for the Dealin 'n Wheelin
Previously Owned Car Company, you might construct records that describe the cars in stock, as follows:

```
type
  years = 1900..1985;
  colors = (black, blue, green, red, white, yellow);
  astring = record
              a: array[1..30] of char;
              numchar: 0..30
            end;
  modelrecord = record
                  name: astring;
                  year: years;
                  color: colors
                end;
  makerecord = record
                 name: astring;
                 address: astring;
                 model: modelrecord
               end;
  manufacrecord = record
                    name: astring;
                    country: astring;
                    make: makerecord
                  end;
  carrecord = record
                manufacturer: manufacrecord;
                regnum: astring;
                price: real
              end;
var
  stock: array[1..1000] of carrecord;
```

But to refer to the year of the ith car in stock, you would then have to write the expression stock[i].manufacturer.make.model.year, which is unnecessarily complicated. See Fig. 2.5.

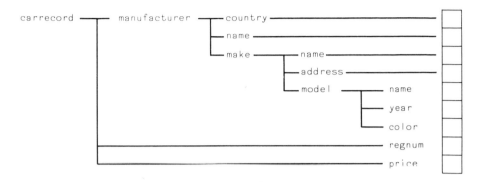

Figure 2.5 Complex record structure.

The car record could be declared more simply, as follows:

```
type
   years = 1900..1985;
   colors = (black, blue, green, red, white, yellow);
   astring = record
                a: array[1..30] of char;
                numchar: 0..30
             end;
   carrecord = record
                manufacturer, country, make, address,
                   model, regnum: astring;
                year: years;
                color: colors;
                price: real
             end;
var
   stock: array[1..1000] of carrecord;
```

The year of the ith car in stock can then be written much more simply as stock[i].year. See Fig. 2.6.

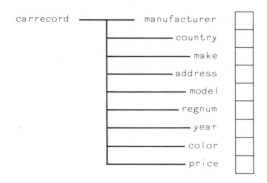

Figure 2.6 Simple record structure.

13 Enumeration expresses intention.

With the exception of variables used for input or output, subrange and enumeration[7] types should be used to restrict the possible values of your variables. Use of subrange and enumeration types takes the burden of range checking off the programmer (that means you!) and puts it on the compiler. It also improves the readability and understandability of your program because it tells your reader something about how a particular variable is used.

In your Pascal program you might write type declarations, such as the following:

```
type
    testscores = integer;
    letters    = char;
    digits     = char;
```

Although these declarations would not stop the program from running successfully, they can be rewritten to be more specific and to provide for better error checking. Because a test score is usually an integer between 0 and 100, a letter is one of the characters *a* to *z*, and a digit is

---

[7]Enumerate—to specify one after the other. Think of an enumeration type as one in which the possible values of a variable are listed one after the other in the declaration.

one of the characters 0 to 9, we can rewrite the declaration to be more specific, as follows:

```
type
    testscores = 0..100;
    letters    = 'a'..'z';
    digits     = '0'..'9';
```

Now, if we declare the variable myscore of type testscores, and we try to make the following assignment,

```
    myscore := 101;
```

then the compiler will stop our program's progress and alert us that we have tried to assign an out-of-range value to the variable myscore. What a pleasure it is to think that the compiler can do some of the error checking for us![8]

14 Remember the structure theorem.

The foundations for structured programming were established in 1966 by Böhm and Jacopini, who proved what we call the "structure theorem." According to this theorem, any computer program can be written using one or more of the three basic control structures: sequence, selection, and iteration.

The sequence is the simplest of the three structures. In the sequence structure (Fig. 2.7), statements are executed one after the other in the order in which they occur. Here is an example of a sequence:

```
    read(x1,y1,x2,y2);
    distance := sqrt(sqr(x1-x2)+sqr(y1-y2));
    write(distance:7:2);
```

---

[8] But be forewarned! We have found some compilers that do not do the range checking that they're supposed to do.

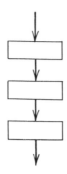

Figure 2.7 Sequence structure.

The selection, or conditional, structure (Fig. 2.8) presents a condition and then selects one of two choices, depending on whether the condition is true or false. The **if-then-else** statement in Pascal is a selection structure. In the following example, such a structure is used to print whether or not x is larger than y. We discuss the selection structure in more detail in Proverb 15.

```
if x > y   then
    writeln(x, ' is larger than ', y)
else
    writeln(x, ' is not larger than ' y);
```

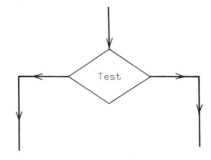

Figure 2.8 Selection structure.

The iteration structure (Fig. 2.9) causes a set of instructions to be executed repeatedly as long as a given condition holds. In Pascal the **while-do** statement is an iteration structure, as are the **repeat-until** and the **for-to-do** statements. Note that the iteration structure has only a single entry and a single exit. In the following example, such a structure is used to print the integers from 1 to 100. We discuss the iteration structure in more detail in Proverb 16.

```
x := 0;
while x < 100 do
    begin
        x := x + 1;
        writeln(x:3)
    end;
```

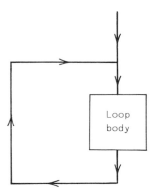

Figure 2.9 Iteration structure.

In 1968 Professor Edsger Dijkstra of the Technological University of Eindhoven, the Netherlands, wrote a letter to the editor of the *Communications of the ACM*, a publication of the Association for Computer Machinery, titled "Go To Statement Considered Harmful." In this letter, Professor Dijkstra wrote that the quality of programmers is "a decreasing function of the density of **goto** statements"[9] in their programs. He advocated the removal of the **goto** statement from all high-level languages because it is "an invitation to make a mess of one's program."[9]

Professor Dijkstra was complaining about the very complex control flow that can result from arbitrary use of **goto** statements. Abrupt transfers of control from one part of a program to another make the program hard to read and understand, even for the original programmer and, indeed, increase the risk of error and are often a sign that the programmer did not fully understand what he was doing. Dijkstra contended that if the structure of an algorithm is well understood, the sequence, selection, and iteration structures suffice to produce a program that is efficient and easily understood.

Unfortunately, some people equate structured programming with the elimination of **goto**'s. Merely removing the **goto**'s from a poorly structured program can make a bad situation worse. Structured programming involves much more than "**goto**-less" programming. It begins with a well-understood structured design, which should lead very naturally to a well-structured implementation constructed from the sequence, selection, and iteration structures. As a consequence of the better understanding that follows from the structured design, **goto** statements become unnecessary. We will discuss the **goto** statement and its role in structured programming again in Proverb 17.

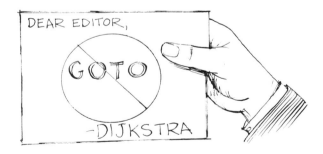

---

[9]Edsger W. Dijkstra, "Go to statement considered harmful." *Communications of the ACM* 11:3 (1968), p. 147. Reprinted with the permission of the Association of Computing Machinery.

15 Consider the conditions for using conditionals.

The conditional, or selection, structures decide or select what action to perform under a certain circumstance or condition. In Pascal, the conditional, or selection, structures take the form of the **if-then-else** and **case** statements. Now let's consider the conditions under which we would use these conditional structures.

The **if-then-else** statement should be used when exactly one of two distinct and mutually exclusive[10] alternative actions is to be performed. Consider the following fragment:

```
if hoursworked <= 40 then
    computeregularpay;
if hoursworked >= 40 then
    computeovertimepay;
```

If this piece of code were actually used, those people who worked exactly 40 hours a week would receive a double paycheck! In place of the above code, the following **if-then-else** statement should be used:

```
if hoursworked <= 40 then
    computeregularpay
else
    computeovertimepay;
```

But if action is to be taken only if the boolean expression[11] is true, then the **if-then** statement should be used in place of the **if-then-else** statement. Consider the following fragment:

```
if hoursworked > 0 then
    computepay
else;
```

---

[10]Mutually exclusive—either alternative may be selected but not both.

[11]Boolean expression—an expression that takes on the value true or false. In the previous example, hoursworked <= 40 is a boolean expression.

Although the previous statement is syntactically correct, the **else** in this statement is a red herring and serves no useful purpose. The compiler sees an empty statement following the **else** and does nothing. The statement is better written as an **if-then** statement without the **else**. For more information, see Proverb 29 for a discussion of the null **else** and dangling **else**.

On the other hand, if we must consider a number of distinct values of one variable, each value associated with a different action, then the **case** statement is more appropriate than a long succession of **else-if** alternatives. For example, instead of

```
if classification = programmer then
   salary := 26000
else if classification = systemsanalyst then
   salary := 34000
else if classification = salesrepresentative then
   salary := 28000
else if classification = marketinganalyst then
   salary := 36000
else if classification = manager then
   salary := 46000;
```

a **case** statement should be used:

```
case classification of
   programmer: salary := 26000;
   systemsanalyst: salary := 34000;
   salesrepresentative: salary := 28000;
   marketinganalyst: salary := 36000;
   manager: salary := 46000
end; (* Case classification *)
```

The **case** statement expresses the alternatives more clearly and concisely than a long, complicated **if-then-else** statement.

However, if you need to protect a condition, then a succession of if-then's is appropriate. For example,

```
if  y <> 0 then
    if  x/y < 1 then
```

But if no part of a compound condition need be protected, then you may use boolean operators. For example,

```
if  (y <> 0) and (x * y < 1) then
```

In summary, implement

- Selection of one of two alternatives with if-then-else.

- Optional selection of one alternative with if-then.

- Selection of one of three or more alternatives with the case statement, which is preferable where possible, or alternatively with if .. then .. else if .. then ..

- Protected conditions with if .. then if .. then ..

16 Take a while to terminate.

Of the various iteration structures in Pascal (the for, while, and repeat loops), the for loop is the least flexible; it is useful only if you know exactly how many times the statements within the loop are to be executed. The while and repeat loops, which are more general and more powerful alternatives to the for loop, use boolean conditions to control continued execution or immediate termination. The statements within a while loop are executed after the condition is tested, whereas the statements in a repeat loop are executed before the condition is tested. Thus, the body of a while loop may never be executed, whereas the body of a repeat loop is executed at least once (see Fig. 2.10).

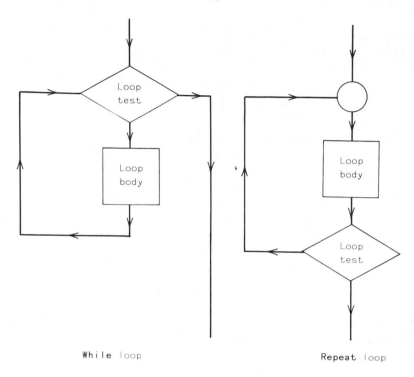

While loop   Repeat loop

Figure 2.10 Difference between the **while** and **repeat** loops.

In the following example we search for an element, called the key, in an array. We introduce the boolean variable **found** and terminate the **repeat** loop when the key is found.

```
(* Search an array a for the key element. *)
found := false;
i := 1;
repeat
  if a[i] = key then
    found := true
  else
    i := i + 1
until (i > n) or found;
```

Because the test is performed after the statements are executed, this **repeat** loop fails if the array is empty. A **while** loop should be used instead, so that the test is performed before entering the loop the first time, as follows:

```
(* Search an array a for the key element. *)
found := false;
i := 1;
while (i <= n) and not found do
  if a[i] = key then
    found := true
  else
    i := i + 1;
```

Generally speaking, it's best to rephrase **repeat** loops as **while** loops to minimize the risk of error.

17 Goto's get you nowhere.

Goto's can lead to logic errors and can make code much more difficult to read, especially if they are used to jump backwards, to implement several alternative exits from a loop, or are used too often. If you find yourself using more than a few **goto**'s, then you have failed to understand the proper use of the Pascal control structures. Rather than **goto**'s, use loops, conditionals, and subprograms instead.

To illustrate the point, let's suppose that Willie Liker, owner of the Fly-by-Night Computer Dating Service, needs a program written to help

him run his business. Willie has devised a questionnaire that requires yes/no responses. He matches a female and a male if they give exactly the same response to all of his questions. The first question he asks is

Do you like to hold hands on the first date?

We set up a boolean array `femaleresponses` such that the response to the `i`th question is contained in `femaleresponses[i]` for the particular female who is being considered. For example, `femaleresponses[1]` = `true` means that the female likes to hold hands on the first date, whereas `femaleresponses[1]` = `false` means that she would prefer that her new date keep his hands to himself. A similar array of responses is set up for the male.

We want to find a pair of arrays such that `femaleresponses[i]` matches `maleresponses[i]` for each `i`. We assume that Mr. Liker's business is so successful that if he keeps looking, he will be able to match each female who requests a date with a compatible male. The wrong way to solve this problem is as follows:

```
(* In this fragment we are looking for a date for   *)
(* a particular female client.  We continue looking *)
(* at prospective males, knowing that eventually    *)
(* we'll find a match.                              *)

        getnextfemale(femalename, femaleresponses);
30:     getnextmale(malename, maleresponses);
        for i := 1 to numquestions do
          begin
            if femaleresponses[i] then
              goto 10;
            if not maleresponses[i] then
              goto 20;
            goto 30;
10:         if not maleresponses[i] then
              goto 30
20:       end;
```

The preceding fragment is an example of "spaghetti" programming in which the **goto** statements are intertwined among themselves. The logic is very difficult to follow. The fragment is much more clearly written, without the use of **goto**'s, as follows:

```
(* In this fragment we are looking for a date for    *)
(* a particular female client.  We continue looking *)
(* at prospective males, knowing that eventually     *)
(* we'll find a match.                               *)

(* Request the name and data of a female client.     *)
    getnextfemale(femalename, femaleresponses);

(* Get the information for a male candidate.          *)
    getnextmale(malename, maleresponses);

(* Run through the responses to see if the client    *)
(* and the male candidate match.                     *)
i := 1;
while i <= numquestions do
  if femaleresponses[i] = maleresponses[i] then
    i := i + 1
  else
    begin
    (* Male does not match, so ask for a new    *)
    (* male candidate.                          *)
      getnextmale(malename, maleresponses);
      i := 1
    end;
```

There are, however, a few very special circumstances in which the **goto** statement is useful. A **goto** can be helpful for handling errors or other abnormalities in logic. Here is an example in which using a **goto** for error handling is appropriate. Suppose, for some reason, you need to write a subprogram that adds up all of the components of a given three-dimensional matrix. If any one of the components is negative, then you want to print an error message that the matrix is rejected. Let's see how this might be done.

```
(* If each entry is non-negative, find the sum of *)
(* the entries in the three-dimensional matrix a. *)
(* Otherwise, reject the entire matrix and return *)
(* to the calling program.                        *)
procedure findsum(var a: matrix; var sum: integer);
label 999;
var
  i: 1..imax;
  j: 1..jmax;
  k: 1..kmax;
begin
  sum := 0;
  for i := 1 to imax do
    for j := 1 to jmax do
      for k := 1 to kmax do
        (* If value is negative, reject entire matrix. *)
        if a[i,j,k] < 0 then
          begin
            writeln('a[', i:2, ',', j:2, ',', k:2, '] =',
                    a[i,j,k], ' is negative.');
            writeln('The matrix is rejected.');
            goto 999 (*Jump out of loop to end of routine*)
          end
        else
          sum := sum + a[i,j,k];
999: (* 999 labels a null statement. *)
end; (* Procedure findsum *)
```

Notice that the **goto** is used to terminate this procedure because of an error in the matrix. The **goto**, in this case, is an effective way to handle the transfer of control when we need to jump through a number of levels. Notice also how we carefully commented the **goto** statement. Trying to follow uncommented **goto** statements can be very confusing.

Always be careful during those limited occasions when you need to use **goto**'s. If you find that you need to handle an abnormal condition, error, or break in the normal program flow, then you may use a **goto**. Under all other conditions, avoid the use of the **goto** statement.

18 Structure needs a framework first.

In Proverbs 9 and 10, we discussed a structured approach to problem solving and tools for structured programming. A structured program is divided up into logical blocks and includes subprograms (i.e., procedures and functions) that correspond to the problems and subproblems to be solved. Each high-level procedure or function uses lower-level procedures and functions to handle the details of its computations. The statement block of the main program, which is at the highest level, consists primarily of calls to these procedures and functions.

A structured program needs a framework, and in building a framework for your program you will want to write the statement block of the main program first. Postpone writing the details of the procedures and functions until later, after the main program is written. When you use a procedure or function, first determine the interfaces, that is, the parameters that are passed into and returned by the procedure or function. Make the procedure or function fit the calling program, rather than the other way around.

It is hard to test, or even to compile, your program if the procedures and functions have not yet been written. Therefore, the framework of a program is built using stubs. A stub is a preliminary, simplified version of a procedure or function that allows computation and execution to proceed, so that higher-level procedures and functions can be tested. It may do nothing more than write a message that a particular procedure or function has been reached. It must, however, return a value in each of its out parameters to the calling program. Sometimes it will request the programmer to type in a suitable value. Not until later is the stub expanded into a complete procedure or function. A stub is quite a good specification of a procedure or function because it is highly designed around the "in" and "out" parameters of the procedure or function.

The following is an example of a stub for a procedure that computes the determinant of a square matrix. Such a procedure might be used in solving a system of linear equations. (For more information on determinants, you may wish to take a course in linear algebra.) Notice that this stub prints a message that the procedure has been reached. It also assigns a value to each of its out parameters.

```
(* This procedure computes the determinant of  *)
(* a square matrix and returns its value along *)
(* with a flag, which indicates whether the    *)
(* determinant is zero or not.                 *)
procedure finddeterminant(var a: matrix;
      var determinant: real; var nonzero: boolean);
begin
  writeln('Finddeterminant has been entered.');
  determinant := 1;
  nonzero := true
end;
```

We can test other higher-level procedures using this stub, and add the actual code for computing the determinant later. Stubs enable us to test the general structure of a program. We can see whether the procedures and functions are called in the right order and whether the data being passed into the procedures and functions are correct. You'll find a more thorough discussion of stubs in Proverb 77.

As you develop the framework for your program, you will also need to consider the placement of your procedures and functions. Procedures and functions that are used throughout your code (for instance, those that build the abstract data types described in Proverb 11) should be grouped together at the main program level because they logically go together. On the other hand, procedures and functions that serve, in terms of the top-down design, as refinements to other routines should be located within the routine that they expand upon. Your programs will be much clearer if you group together procedures and functions that are logically or conceptually related.

19 Do one thing at a time, and do it well, but don't be seen doing it.

Instead of writing the same block of code more than once, you can avoid duplication of effort and make your program easier to read and understand by using procedures and functions. Procedures and functions should be looked at as little black boxes that do a special task. Thus, they fit right in with the idea of information hiding, which we've already considered in Proverb 11.

Once you build and test a black box, you don't have to rebuild it, and you can depend on it to do the work that it was designed to do. You simply call on the black box to do its work and then return control of the task to you when it is finished. You don't need to know about the mechanism hidden in the black box. All you need to know is what the black box will do for you when you call it into action.

One day, Phyllis, who owns and operates Phyllis's Physical Fitness Farm, was designing a program to compute the mean, or average, weights of her clients before and after they engaged in her diet and exercise program, and also their mean height. First, Phyllis wrote the following piece of code:

```
(* Compute the means of the weights and heights. *)

totalwtbefore := 0;
for i := 1 to n do
  totalwtbefore := totalwtbefore + weightbefore[i];
meanwtbefore := totalwtbefore/n;

totalwtafter := 0;
for i := 1 to n do
  totalwtafter := totalwtafter + weightafter[i];
meanwtafter := totalwtafter/n;

totalheight := 0;
for i := 1 to n do
  totalheight := totalheight + height[i];
meanheight := totalheight/n;
```

But she quickly discovered that her code would have been easier to write and read if she had first written a function that finds the mean of an arbitrary collection of numbers. After performing a few mental gymnastics, she rewrote her code as follows:

```
(* This function accepts an array a and an      *)
(* integer n and returns the mean, or average, *)
(* of the first n components of a.              *)

function mean(a: numberarray; n: nonnegint): real;
var
   total: real;
   i: nonnegint;
begin
   total := 0;
   for i := 1 to n do
      total := total + a[i];
   mean := total/n
end; (* Function mean *)
```

Phyllis's code is not only more readable, but it makes the job easier for her because she can simply call the function whenever she needs to find a mean. Thus, in the main program she would write

```
(* Compute the means of the weights and heights. *)

meanwtbefore := mean(weightbefore, n);
meanwtafter := mean(weightafter, n);
meanheight := mean(height, n);
```

20 Hard to detect is a side effect.

A side effect is said to occur when a global variable is modified by a procedure or function or when a function modifies one of its own parameters. Such side effects can cause problems because use of the procedure or function provides no indication to the user that the global variable will be modified, and an error may result from the assumption that it remains unchanged. The error can be quite difficult to detect. To prevent unexpected side effects, parameters and local variables (rather than global variables) should be used in procedures and functions. Take a look at the following example:

```
(* This program demonstrates a side-effect that  *)
(* occurs when the global variable g is modified *)
(* by the function s.                            *)

program sideeffects(input, output);
var
   g: integer;
function s(x: integer): integer;
begin
   s := x + g;
   g := g + 1
end;

begin
   g := 0;
   writeln(s(0):5, s(0):5, s(0):5, s(0):5, s(0).5)
end.
```

Looking at the writeln statement in which the function s is called five times, you might expect the same value s(0) to be printed five times because no reference is made to the global variable g. However, the value of g is incremented by 1 each time the function is called, and the output of this program is

0   1   2   3   4

Do you see why? Run through the program by hand to convince yourself of this. As you can see from this example, making changes to global variables within procedures and functions can be misleading. You should take special care to note any side effects that may occur.

21 Parameters are in and out; globals should be out of sight.

To prevent unexpected and undesired side effects, use parameters rather than global variables in your procedures and functions. Avoid using global variables—use parameters instead. Think of your procedure

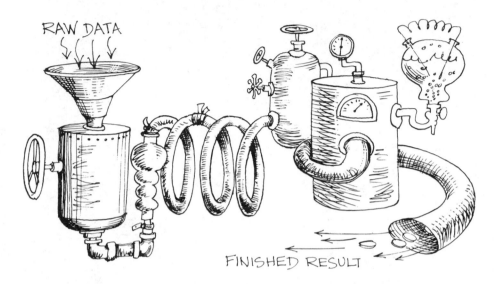

RAW DATA

FINISHED RESULT

or function as a machine that accepts raw data, which it uses to produce and return a finished result. Pass the raw data, by means of parameters, into your procedures and functions, and pass the finished result back out to the calling program by means of parameters of the procedure or the name of the function. By passing all of the information on which the result depends as parameters into the procedure or function, we make that dependence explicit and avoid unfortunate errors.

Consider Randy Kruger, a manufacturer of gold coins and medallions, who uses a computer to calculate the weights of his coins.

```
(* This function computes the weight *)
(* of a coin given its diameter and  *)
(* thickness.                        *)
function weight(diameter, thickness: inches): ounces;
var
   radius: inches;
begin
   radius := diameter/2;
   weight := 3.14159*sqr(radius)*thickness*densityofgold
end;
```

Note that the density of gold is accessed as a global variable, which might have sufficed had not Randy decided for reasons of economy to manufacture certain coins from lead rather than gold. He forgot that his weight function depended implicitly, but not explicitly, on the density of gold. (This led to Randy's "vacationing" in Leavenworth rather than Copacabana.) Had he written

```
(* This function computes the weight *)
(* of a coin given its diameter and  *)
(* thickness.                        *)

function weight(diameter, thickness: inches;
                density: ouncepercubicinch): ounces;
var
   radius: inches;
begin
   radius := diameter/2;
   weight := 3.14159*sqr(radius)*thickness*density
end;
```

he might have noticed that he should call

```
            weight(diam, thick, densityoflead);
```

rather than

```
            weight(diam, thick, densityofgold);
```

Global variables should be used in procedures or functions only for data that are invisible to the code that is calling the procedure or function. An example of a variable that is invisible might be a variable used to count how often a procedure or function is called; such a count can be useful for improving performance or for calculating charges. Another kind of invisible variable might provide resources for use by a program, such as a pool of buffers.[12] A further possibility might be a variable that is designed not to affect the result of a calculation but, rather, to speed

---

[12]Buffer—an intermediate storage place for data. A pool of buffers is several of such storage places.

the calculation by recording the results of previous calculations. For example, B. Tree, the designer of the Cornucopia of Knowledge Information Retrieval System, noticed that her users rather frequently requested the same information repeatedly. Consequently, she wrote

```
procedure find(key: index; var rec: inforecord);
begin
  if key = lastkey then
    rec := lastrec
  else
    .
    .
    .
end;
```

where lastkey and lastrec are global variables, invisible to the user except in speed of response.

When passing parameters to a procedure, we must consider the use to be made of them. Some of our parameters are used only to pass a value into the procedure; we might call these "in" parameters. Other parameters are used only for passing a result back out of the procedure; these might be called "out" parameters. There are parameters whose value is read in by the procedure, modified, and passed back out; these are the "in-out" parameters. Always decide whether your parameters are in, out, or in-out.

Pascal provides two parameter modes: value and reference. A value parameter is like a local variable of a procedure. When the procedure is called, the value of the actual parameter is calculated, and that value is copied into the value parameter. Reference parameters (sometimes also called variable parameters or **var** parameters) are indicated by the reserved word **var** preceding the parameter declaration. A reference parameter is like a pointer variable. When the procedure is called, the address of the actual parameter is calculated, and that address is copied into the reference parameter; thus, the reference parameter points to where the data are located in memory.

Accessing a value parameter is generally much quicker and more efficient than access through a reference parameter. You might therefore be tempted to always use value parameters. But updating a value parameter will have no effect on the original source from which that value was copied. Consequently, value parameters are only useful for in parameters. For out and in-out parameters, we must always use reference (or **var**) parameters.

We must be careful even with in parameters. An array can be quite large, and copying it can waste a lot of time and storage space. Consequently, for arrays and also for large records, it's better to use reference parameters even for in parameters. Reference parameters must always be used when passing files as parameters.

Now let's consider the following example in which we intend to interchange the values of x and y.

```
procedure swap(x, y: integer);
var
   temp: integer;
begin
   temp := x;
   x := y;
   y := temp
end;
```

The procedure swap shown above will not work as you might expect. Because x and y are passed as value parameters, rather than reference parameters, they will not be interchanged by the procedure swap. The correction in this case is very simple. All we have to do is insert **var** before x and y in the procedure heading.

```
procedure swap(var x, y: integer);
var
   temp: integer;
begin
   temp := x;
   x := y;
   y := temp
end;
```

Do you understand why?   Generally speaking, if you want a parameter to be changed by a procedure or function, make it a reference parameter; otherwise, make it a value parameter.

22 Local variables are temporary variables; make temporary variables local.

Temporary variables should be declared as local variables within the procedure or function in which they are used and not in the main program. The reason why local variables should be used rather than global variables is that local variables eliminate side effects and minimize errors that might result from the interaction of two or more subprograms.

Suppose, for example, that total has been declared as a global variable and is used within a function that finds the sum of the entries in a particular column of a matrix.

```
(* This function finds the sum of the entries *)
(* in a particular column of a matrix.        *)

function columntotal(var a: matrix;
                        col, rowsize: subscript): real;
var
  i: subscript;
begin
  total := 0;
  for i := 1 to rowsize do
    total := total + a[i,col];
  columntotal := total
end;
```

Each time this function is called, the value of total will be modified. If the variable total is used for some other purpose in the main program, this could cause a serious problem. The function should be rewritten so that the temporary variable total is declared locally, as follows:

```
(* This function finds the sum of the entries *)
(* in a particular column of a matrix. .      *)

function columntotal(var a: matrix;
                     col, rowsize: subscript): real;
var
   total: real;
   i: subscript;
begin
   total := 0;
   for i := 1 to rowsize do
     total := total + a[i,col];
   columntotal := total
end;
```

A second reason for using local variables rather than global variables is to make more efficient use of memory. The memory space that is used by the local variables of a procedure or function is used only while the procedure or function is executing—it is allocated when the procedure or function is called and freed when control is returned to the calling program. Memory required by global variables, on the other hand, is allocated for the entire time your program is executing.

Because memory space used by local variables of a procedure or function is allocated only while the procedure or function is executing, local variables do not retain their values between calls. Local variables are temporary variables, and temporary variables should be declared as local variables to eliminate side effects and minimize errors, and to make more efficient use of memory.

Problems and Projects

1. The *ACM Computing Surveys* is a journal that contains articles of a tutorial nature. The December 1974 issue (Vol. 6, No. 4) is a special issue on programming. Go to your library and read this issue. Then write a one- or two-page report on one of the articles you have read.

2. Write a type declaration for a data structure that can be used to store information about

   (a) The books in a library.

   (b) Cards in a deck of playing cards.

   (c) A lot of rental cars.

   (d) Listings in a telephone directory.

   Remember, simple is the sign of skill!

3. Consider, again, the problem of Galactic Business Machines, Inc., in Proverb 9. Refine each of the subproblems of "Process order," as we have done for "Back-order out-of-stock items."

4. Design a flowchart and a data flow diagram to solve a quadratic equation $ax^2 + bx + c = 0$, using the famous formula

$$x = \frac{-b \pm \sqrt{b^2 - 4ac}}{2a}$$

   What are the advantages and disadvantages of each of these tools?

5. Construct a structure chart for

   (a) Writing a term paper.

   (b) Planning and arranging your vacation.

   (c) Moving from one house or apartment to another.

   (d) Planning and giving a Halloween party.

   You may want to read Proverb 10 again.

6. Following the publication of Professor Dijkstra's letter in the March 1968 issue of the *Communications of the ACM*, a series of letters appeared in the *Communications* and also in *Datamation*. Obtain copies of these issues and read the relevant letters. Write a one-page paper that summarizes the opposing views on the use of the `goto` statement.

7. Restructure the following fragment to eliminate all **goto**'s. The fragment is intended to compute square roots. It calls the function max, which you may assume has already been defined.

```
10:  read(x);
      if x >= 0.0 then
         goto 20;
      write('The square root of', x, 'is undefined.');
      goto 10;
20:  if x > 0 then
         goto 30;
      y := 0.0;
      goto 50;
30:  y := 1.0;
40:  z := y;
      y := (x/z + z)/2.0;
      if abs(x/y/y-1.0)/max(x/y/y,1.0) >= 0.000001 then
         goto 40;
50:  write('The square root of ', x, '=', y);
      goto 10;
```

8. Write an automated grading program for your instructor. The program will take as input each student's name and his or her grades on the exams and assignments. Your program will issue "prompts" telling the user what to enter. The output from the program will consist of a "header" line, which labels columns of data. Each line below it will consist of the name of a student, his or her grades on the exams and assignments, and final weighted average grade.

The program will use procedures and functions to do its work. One procedure will print the heading at the top of the class list; another will read a student's name and grades on the exams and assignments; a third will compute the weighted average; and a fourth will print all of the data concerning the particular student. Your program should be capable of handling an arbitrary number of students. Make sure that your program is written in a style (with indentation and comments) that makes the logic of the program easy to follow. This program will be considered again in Chapter 3, Problem 8.

9. Do you understand the difference between value and reference parameters? Look at the following program. What are the values of the variables that are printed when the program is run? If necessary, read Proverb 21 again.

```
program test(input, output);
var
   a, b: integer;
   procedure change(x: integer; var y: integer);
   begin
      x := x + 1;
      y := y - 1;
      writeln('x = ', x);
      writeln('y = ', y)
   end;

begin
   a := 0;
   b := 0;
   change(a, b);
   writeln('a = ', a);
   writeln('b = ', b)
end.
```

10. Dynamic Demographics, Inc., has collected data on the ages of individuals in a sample population. As a programmer for the company, your assignment is to write a program that reads the data into an array and uses procedures and functions to find the mean, the median, and the mode of these ages.

The mean is the average of the values, obtained by summing them up and dividing by the number n of them. The median is the value that occurs in the middle of the array when it is sorted. If the number n is even, then there is no exact middle, and the value just to the left of the middle is taken as the median. The mode is the value that occurs most frequently. If two or more values occur an equal number of times, then the mode is the value that is the largest.

11. In Proverb 22 we discussed global and local variables. With this proverb in mind, consider the following program structure:

```
program main(input, output);
var
  x, y, z: integer;
    procedure proc1(x1, y1: integer);
    var
      z1: integer;
        procedure proc2(y2: integer);
        var
          z2: integer;
        begin (* Proc2 *)

          .

          .

          end;   (* Proc2 *)
    begin (* Proc1 *)

      .

      .

    end;   (* Proc1 *)
    procedure proc3(x3: integer);
    var
      z3: integer;
    begin (* Proc3 *)

      .

      .

    end;   (* Proc3 *)
  begin (* Main *)

    .

    .

  end. (* Main *)
```

Answer true or false to each of the following.

(a) z1 is local to proc1 and global to proc2.

(b) z3 can be accessed by all parts of the program.

(c) z is a global variable that is visible to and can be accessed by all parts of the program, including proc2.

(d) The statement z1 := z2 in the statement block of proc1 would be legal.

(e) proc2 could be called in proc1 with the parameter y1.

12. A ticket agency uses a computerized reservation system for booking rock concert seats. The system makes use of a two-dimensional array a[row,seat], where row is an integer between 1 and 30, and seat is a letter of the alphabet a through z. The value of a component of the array is either u (unreserved) or r (reserved). Create a top-down design for a system having the following operations:

Reserve   makes a reservation, if possible.

Cancel   cancels the reservation.

Adjacent   indicates whether or not there are two adjacent, unreserved seats in a given row.

13. In Proverb 11 we discussed the idea of data abstraction. Go to your library, find a copy of the October 1984 issue of *IEEE Software* (Vol. 1, No. 4), and read the article "Abstraction Techniques in Modern Programming Languages" by Mary Shaw. Write a one-page summary of what you have learned.

14. Write a complete program for Willie Liker's Fly-by-Night Computer Dating Service, dropping the assumption that there is always a matching male for each female. If you have problems making the program work properly, add debugging write statements to assist you in finding the problem (see Proverb 79).

3
Program
Legibility

In both academic and industrial programming enviroments, legibility is an important attribute of well-written programs. Making an effort to produce legible programs pays off at every stage of program development, whether you are creating, debugging, or modifying a program, or just trying to figure out what a particular piece of code does.

The proverbs in this chapter emphasize the importance of writing programs in a straightforward fashion, so that they can be easily read and understood. These proverbs include dos and don'ts of commenting, suggestions for choosing identifiers, recommendations for code layout and indentation, and rules for semicolon placement and use of parentheses. In this chapter you'll also see how symbolic logic can be applied when writing programs to produce more legible code.

Now it's time to pay attention to the stylistic aspects of your programming and to learn how to write readable code.

23 Write only read-easy programs.

Programming is an art! As such, it involves more than just writing programs that do the job; it involves writing programs that are easy to read and easy to understand. Such read-easy programs are written in a clear, direct, simple manner.

Sometimes programmers are tempted to come up with some "gee whiz" way of writing a certain chunk of code. However, remember that if the "whiz" way is more confusing than the simple and direct approach, then the code becomes harder to understand and debug. Therefore, when coding, say what you mean, be simple and direct, and don't sacrifice clarity for small gains in efficiency.

For example, Alexander Smart is charged with measuring the total flow of water down the Amazon River for the benefit of the Pirhana Fishery. Every hour on the hour, Alexander measures the flow, but then he must convert these measurements into a total daily flow.

	0	1	2	3	4	...	22	23	24
Time	12 p.m.	1 a.m.	2 a.m.	3 a.m.	4 a.m.	...	10 p.m.	11 p.m.	12 p.m.
Flow	4694	5732	6147	6467	7329	...	6926	6527	5167

(million gallons per hour)

Alexander decides to use Simpson's Rule to convert his measurements into a daily flow. Simpson's Rule, as applied to his problem states that

$$\text{Daily flow} = \frac{1}{3}[f(0) + 4 \times f(1) + 2 \times f(2) + 4 \times f(3) + 2 \times f(4) +$$

$$... + 2 \times f(22) + 4 \times f(23) + f(24)]$$

We do not try to explain here why the sequence of weights, 1, 4, 2, 4, 2, ... , 2, 4, 1, is appropriate. They look strange, but Simpson's Rule actually gives rather good results. You will probably learn more about Simpson's Rule in your other classes, perhaps calculus or possibly numerical analysis.

To program this calculation, Alexander had to find a way of making his program apply the correct sequence of weights while summing the flows. He concocted the following program:

```
sum := 0;
for  i  := 0 to n do
   sum :=   sum +
            f[i]*(2 + 2*(i mod 2) - 1 div (i+1) - i div n);
dailyflow := 1/3 * sum;
```

That complex expression may be obvious to Smart Aleck, and indeed it computes the correct weights. But nobody else will be able to read the program and understand what it does. A much simpler program would have been more appropriate, such as

```
        sum := 0;
        for i := 0 to n do
           if (i = 0) or (i = n) then
              sum := sum + f[i]
           else if i mod 2 = 1 then
              sum := sum + 4 * f[i]
           else
              sum := sum + 2 * f[i];
        dailyflow := 1/3 * sum;
```

To be sure that you are writing your code simply and clearly, use the "dorm test":

> If one of your classmates standing in the parking lot can understand your code when it's screamed out from a third floor window of your dorm, then it's clear enough. Otherwise, it needs rewriting.

24 Names and natures should agree.

When writing structured programs, keep in mind one of the most important goals: to write readable code. Choose names (i.e., identifiers) for your types, constants, variables, and subprograms that are descriptive of their meaning. Meaningful names, chosen to match the nature of these program entities, provide a clear indication of their purpose in a program. Programming and debugging become easier because it is apparent what they are used for. Best of all, the code is much easier to read.

In writing an inventory program for Wanda's Wardrobes, a retail clothing store, we need to choose a name for a variable that represents the number of daily receipts for the store. We can call it

x

But by the time we get into the middle of the code, this variable will lose its meaning. Instead, we can call it

dr

Although this is a much better choice than x, there are still better choices. We can call it

```
dailyreceipts
```

This is an excellent choice.

Now we also need to write a function that validates the price of each item sold in Wanda's Wardrobes. We could call the function

```
pc        or      vp
```

But there are better choices, such as

```
pricecheck      or        validprice
```

The function heading might be written like this:

```
(* This routine accepts, as input, the item number and *)
(* price of an inventory item for Wanda's Wardrobes.    *)
(* If the item number and price match up in the         *)
(* item-price table, then validprice is set equal to    *)
(* true.  Otherwise, validprice is set equal to false. *)

function validprice(itemnumber: posint;
                    price: real): boolean;
```

Be sure to choose names for your procedures and functions that best describe the use of the routines. Choose names for your variables that make them easy to identify and to use. Here is some additional helpful advice for choosing variable names.

Avoid choosing the same variable name at different levels of your program. For example, if you use the identifier finalresult for a global variable in your main program, don't use finalresult to identify a local variable in one of your procedures or functions. Although the compiler will be able to recognize each, the human can easily become confused.

In large programs written in teams, you have to expect that different people will choose the same name, but it's best to avoid choosing the same name at different levels if you can. Often, a compound name is used in large programs, the first part of which is the name of the procedure or function in which the variable is declared.

It's also best to avoid choosing the same name for formal and actual parameters.[1] This is particularly true when you have nested procedures or functions, four or five levels deep, each one calling down to the next. If, however, you do use the same name for a formal parameter and an actual parameter, you should be aware that although they have the same name, they really stand for two different things.

```
(* This program illustrates the use of global and     *)
(* local variables and formal and actual parameters.  *)
program stufftolearn(input, output);
var
   mydata: integer;                      }————— global variables
   myresult, finalresult: real;

                                         ┌formal parameters
      procedure letslearn(data: integer; var result: real);
      var
         tempresult: real;  }————— local variables
      begin
         .
         .
         .
      end;

begin (* Main program *)
   .
   .
(* Call procedure letslearn. *)
   letslearn(mydata, myresult)
                                  ————— actual parameters
   .
   .
end.
```

---

[1]Formal parameter—a parameter used in the definition of a procedure or function. Actual parameter—a parameter used in a procedure or function call.

Finally, don't forget to include a declaration for a new variable within a procedure or function. Make sure that you have declared all of the variables that you're using at each stage of program development.

25 Code without comment is like a play without words.

Commenting is very important for the readability of code. Comments should be included as a part of your program from the beginning and should reflect your thinking about the problem. When writing code, ask yourself the following questions:

- What part of the problem solution does the segment of code deal with?

- Are there any special conditions under which the segment will not be executed?

Answer these questions with comments. While you are in the middle of writing code, comments may seem obvious and unnecessary. However, if you wait until after the program is written to add comments, your comments will tend to be superficial and inadequate.

As a student, you may question the value of comments, especially when you're just going to turn in the project and then forget about it. However, someday you may work in a professional programming environment where your project will take months to write and will be used for many years. Other programmers may need to read and possibly rewrite the code to meet changed requirements. Without meaningful comments, your code will be difficult to read and will cost you or other programmers a great deal of time figuring out what the code does.

Many professional programming environments require programmers to use strict coding, commenting, and documentation standards to ensure that time will not be wasted when program update or debug time comes. They often have a standard heading that is required in all routines written for a particular software system. Figure 3.1 contains a sample format of a standard heading that might be used by professional programmers in their projects. (You'll find a more complete discussion of documentation in Chapter 11.)

```
1   *** BEGIN PROLOGUE routine name
2   *
3   *--> PROGRAMMER
4   *       name, date (yy mm dd), organization
5   *       more information
6   *
7   *--> PURPOSE
8   *       information
9   *
10  *--> DESCRIPTION
11  *       information
12  *
13  *--> INPUT OR PARAMETERS
14  *       param1  description of the parameter
15  *               continuation of the description
16  *       param2  description of the parameter
17  *               continuation of the description
18  *
19  *--> ARRAYS USED
20  *       array1  description of its use
21  *               continuation of the description
22  *       array2  description of its use
23  *               continuation of the description
24  *
25  *--> ROUTINES CALLED
26  *       name, name, name, name, name
27  *
28  *--> ROUTINES WHICH CALL THIS ROUTINE
29  *       name, name, name, name, name
30  *
31  *--> FURTHER COMMENTS
32  *       cautions, limitations, assumptions, etc.
33  *
34  *** END PROLOGUE routine name
```

Figure 3.1 Sample routine prologue.

Although this may seem like a great deal of commenting for each procedure or function in a program, most systems development groups use such a standard heading for all routines put into the system. Several systems analysts, software engineers, and programmers work together to develop large system programs, and many others work to correct, update, and maintain the programs. The computer programs making up a large software system may consist of several hundred thousand lines of code. Many routines may be written for a particular project and may later need updating or rewriting by other programmers. A detailed routine heading, or prologue, is necessary so that each programmer who reads and modifies the routine can quickly see the purpose and description of any particular routine in the system.

In the remainder of this section, we give a list of dos and don'ts for writing effective comments. You will notice that we have used (* *) for the comments in our code rather than braces { }. We prefer to use (* *), because braces are not available in all character sets.

Do

1. Include comments before program, procedure, and function headings to describe what the program, procedure, or function is going to do. In this way, the reader of your program gets a preview of what is to come.

You may, however, wish to include these comments after the headings. Some systems are set up to print a program, procedure, or function heading at the top of a page. If a comment is included before the heading, it will not occur on the same page as the program, procedure, or function with which it is associated but, rather, on the bottom of the previous page. Even without such problems, some programming professionals prefer, for stylistic reasons, to include comments after, rather than before, the headings of their programs, procedures, and functions.

When you are writing a program as a class project, you should include your name, the course and section number, your instructor's name, the date, the assignment and/or version number, a brief description of the program, and any necessary background information, such as algorithms and references, that you use. For example,

```
(* Programmer    :   Ima Whizkid                          *)
(* Course        :   Programming Methods                  *)
(*                   CS 2700  Section 1                   *)
(* Instructor    :   Professor I. M. Smart                *)
(* Date          :   February 14, 1985                    *)
(* Assignment 3  :   The Bank Statement                   *)
(*                                                        *)
(* This program accepts as input the monthly deposits *)
(* and withdrawals of a particular banking customer.  *)
(* The program processes the banking data and outputs *)
(* a monthly bank statement complete with beginning   *)
(* and ending account balances for both savings and   *)
(* checking accounts.                                 *)

program bankstatement(input, output);
```

It is also important to comment procedure and function headings. For example, suppose you are writing a Pascal procedure to find the roots of a quadratic equation. The proper way to comment the procedure heading is to include a statement that describes what the procedure does.

```
(* This procedure accepts parameters a, b and c of    *)
(* a quadratic equation ax² + bx + c = 0 and returns  *)
(* the roots, xroot1 and xroot2.  If the roots are    *)
(* imaginary, a message is printed to that effect.    *)
(* If a = 0, then the equation is not quadratic and   *)
(* an error message is printed.                       *)

procedure quadratic(a, b, c: real;
                var xroot1, xroot2: real);
```

2. Include comments in the declaration blocks of your program to explain what the variables are used for, if this is not obvious from the choice of variable names.

```
var
    x1, x2: real; (* x1 and x2 are roots of   *)
                  (* a quadratic equation.    *)
```

3. Use comments to announce what is about to be done and to identify logically related segments of your program. Blank lines can be added to set off these logically related segments from the surrounding program. For example,

```
(* This is the data input validation section. *)

writeln('Input a, the coefficient of x-squared.');
readln(a);

(* Continue reading a until a is different from 0. *)
while a = 0 do
   begin
      writeln('The value of a must be different ',
               'from 0.  You entered a = ', a:7:2);
      writeln('Please input a again.');
      readln(a)
   end;

writeln('Input b, the coefficient of x.');
readln(b);

writeln('Input c, the constant term.');
readln(c);

writeln('Validation completed with a = ', a:7:2,
         ', b = ', b:7:2, ', and c = ', c:7:2);
```

4. Write your comments in simple English. After all, comments are there to clarify code, not to make it confusing. Here is an example of a confusing comment:

```
(* Search for the binary *)
(* bit pattern 1100100.  *)
```

The programmer should have written what he actually meant.

```
(* Look for the integer 100 which *)
(* marks the end of the data set. *)
```

5. Use a comment with each **end**. When programs are longer than a few lines, there are often several end's in the code. Label each **end** to clarify what it terminates. For example,

```
case lightcolor of
   red    : begin
               stopthecar := true;
               keepgoing := false
            end; (* red *)
   yellow : becautious := true;
   green  : begin
               stopthecar := false;
               keepgoing := true
            end (* green *)
end; (* Case lightcolor *)
```

6. Make sure that comments and code agree. Incorrect comments are worse than no comments at all, so be sure to update comments when you change the code. Take a look at this:

```
(* Test for odd numbers. *)

if n mod 2 = 0 then
   evennumber := evennumber + 1;
```

The comment should have read

```
(* Test for even numbers. *)
```

Here is another example. Can you see what is wrong with it?

```
(* Test for deltay.     *)
(* If less than 1.0E-8, *)
(* print error message. *)

epsilon := 1.0E-8;
if deltay <= epsilon then
   writeln('Error: deltay must be greater than ',
            epsilon);
```

The comment should have read

```
(* Test for deltay.  If less than or equal *)
(* to 1.0E-8, print error message.         *)
```

It should have taken you only a few seconds to see this mistake. Although mistakes in your code will not always be obvious, it should be obvious that incorrect comments can cause a great deal of difficulty!

Don't

1. Undercomment. Comments can help others understand your program and help you remember what you meant by something you wrote long ago.

2. Overcomment. The actual program statements may become difficult to read if you have too many comments. Don't use comments to restate the obvious purpose of a program statement. Comments should be used to tell what something is or why something is being done, not how it is being done. Beginning programmers sometimes put comments in their code that give no more information than the actual program statements themselves. Here is an example of overcommented code:

```
(* Read in a value for number. *)
readln(number);

(* If number is negative *)
if number < 0 then
    (* Write an error message. *)
    writeln('Error on input.');
```

3. Finally, don't comment bad code. If you find that your code is very confusing to explain, find a better algorithm or reorganize and rewrite the code, so that it is easier to explain and understand. Most importantly, treat your comments as you would the actual executable program statements. Be careful as you write them and make them meaningful. Although they will not affect the program's execution, they will make changes or corrections much easier and more efficient for you and your fellow programmers.

26 You need space to read the code.

To improve the readability of your program, avoid cramped code. Instead, spread it out to highlight the various blocks of code. Blank lines may be used to separate blocks of code, or blocks of code may be highlighted with asterisks (but don't overdo this!)

As an example, consider the following program, which sorts an array of strings using a sorting algorithm known as Bubblesort. The program needs additional comments, which you are asked to provide in Problem 2 at the end of this chapter.

```
(***********************************************************)
(*                                                       *)
(*      This program reads in a list of names,           *)
(*      sorts the names into alphabetical order,         *)
(*      and prints the alphabetized list.                *)
(*                                                       *)
(***********************************************************)
program sortarray(input, output);
type
   index1 = 1..100;
   index2 = 1..30;
   stringarray = array[index1,index2] of char;
var
   names: stringarray;
   numnames: index1;

(***********************************************************)
procedure readnames(var names: stringarray;
                    var numnames: index1);
var
   i: 1..101;
   j: 1..31;
```

```pascal
(*************************************************)
procedure initializestrings(var names: stringarray);
var
  i: index1;
  j: index2;
begin (* Initializestrings *)
  for i := 1 to 100 do
    for j := 1 to 30 do
      names[i,j] := ' '
end; (* Initializestrings *)

(*************************************************)
begin (* Readnames *)
  initializestrings(names);
  writeln('Enter the names, each on a separate line, ',
          'last name first.');
  writeln('Each name can have at most 30 characters, ',
          'and at most 100 names can be input.');
  writeln;
  i := 1;
  while not eof and (i <= 100) do
    begin
      j := 1;
      while not eoln and (j <= 30) do
        begin
          read(names[i,j]);
          j := j + 1
        end;
      readln;
      i := i + 1
    end;
  numnames := i - 1
end; (* Readnames *)
```

```
(**********************************************************)
procedure writenames(var names: stringarray;
                         numnames: index1);
var
  i: index1;
  j: index2;
begin (* Writenames *)
  writeln('The alphabetized list of names is:');
  for i := 1 to numnames do
    begin
      for j := 1 to 30 do
        write(names[i,j]);
      writeln
    end
end; (* Writenames *)

(**********************************************************)
procedure alphabetize(var names: stringarray;
                        numnames: index1);
var
  i, last: index1;

    (**************************************************)
    procedure swap(rowi, rowj: index1;
                   var a: stringarray);
    var
      temp: char;
      k: index2;
    begin (* Swap *)
      for k := 1 to 30 do
        begin
          temp := a[rowi,k];
          a[rowi,k] := a[rowj,k];
          a[rowj,k] := temp
        end
    end; (* Swap *)
```

```
(*************************************************)

    function greaterthan(rowi, rowj: index1;
                         var a: stringarray): boolean;
    var
      stillequal: boolean;
      k: index2;
    begin (* Greaterthan *)
      stillequal := true;
      k := 1;
      while stillequal and (k <= 30) do
        if a[rowi,k] <> a[rowj,k] then
          stillequal := false
        else
          k :- k + 1;
      if a[rowi,k] > a[rowj,k] then
        greaterthan := true
      else
        greaterthan := false
    end; (* Greaterthan *)

    (*************************************************)

begin (* Alphabetize *)
  for last := numnames downto 2 do
    for i := 1 to last - 1 do
      if greaterthan(i,i+1,names) then
        swap(i,i+1,names)
end; (* Alphabetize *)

(**************************************************)

begin (* Main program *)
  readnames(names,numnames);
  alphabetize(names,numnames);
  writenames(names,numnames)
end. (* Main program *)

(**************************************************)
```

POORLY COMMENTED CODE
CAN COME BACK TO HAUNT YOU!

As a rule of thumb, it's a good idea to leave one blank line before `label`, `const`, `type`, and `var` declarations and three blank lines before procedure and function declarations. Leave one space before and after := and = and one space after : . Use the English rule of spacing between words and symbols, such as +, −, ∗, /, `mod`, `div`, etc. Remember, you need space to read the code!

27 Indent to indicate intent.

Appropriate indentation improves the readability of your program and highlights its logical structure. Although it may not seem of particular importance to a beginning programmer working on short code, indenting to improve readability is very important, and beginners should develop good structuring habits early on. These habits will help you to write logically correct programs and will make them easier for you and others to read and debug. Future employers will especially appreciate your ability to write programs that are easy to read and debug.

A reader (the person who grades the homework assignments) for a course in programming methods at one university encouraged programming students to be concerned with writing readable code by presenting them with the following code fragment:

```
if codeispretty then
  begin
    easytoread := true;
    easiertounderstand := true;
    professional := true
  end
else
    frustratedreader := true;
```

We know what generally happens if the reader for a programming course becomes frustrated! The program listing is returned with a lot of red marks, and the grade assigned is not what the student had hoped for. Nevertheless, when the instructor, the reader, and your text offer you advice on making your program more readable, they are helping you to develop a style that will improve your programs.

You should be particularly careful to make your indentations correspond to the way the computer handles the program logic. Pascal is structured in levels, and the level of a statement is indicated by indenting it. Indentation is especially important when there are multiple levels of nested logic.

For example, compound `if` statements can easily be laid out in a manner that is different from the way in which the computer processes them. Look at the following fragment that helps Stanley Sportsnut decide what to do at a given time of the day:

```
if day = saturday then
  if sunisup then
    gotoballgame := true
else
    godancing := true;
```

The layout of this fragment leads the reader to believe that if it is not Saturday, then Stanley should go dancing. The computer, however, will not interpret the fragment in that way. It will be interpreted as follows: If it is Saturday and the sun is up, then Stanley should go to the ball game; but if it is Saturday and the sun is not up, then Stanley should go out dancing. The appropriate layout is

```
if day = saturday then
   if sunisup then
      gotoballgame := true
   else
      godancing := true;
```

The two pieces of code above will be executed in exactly the same way. Indentation cannot be used to force a meaning on the computer, and improper indentation can confuse a reader. To resolve any doubt about meaning, be explicit about your intent, even if it means being redundant.

When you write your programs, make the layout match the structure of your program and be consistent about indentation within a program. Decide, early on, how the **if-then-else** and other blocks in your program will look. In place of what we have written above, some programmers prefer to write

```
if codeispretty
   then
      .

      .

   else
      .

      .
```

Whichever form you choose, standardize so that the form is consistent throughout your program. Be advised, however, that when you go to work for a particular firm, they may have local programming standards that they expect all of their programmers to follow. Ask your instructor or reader whether there are any special standards required for your programming class.

Here are some helpful hints for indenting to improve the legibility of your programs.

- Line up the `begin-end`, `repeat-until`, `case-end`, and `if-then-else` blocks to emphasize the levels of nested logic. That is, make an `end` line up with its corresponding `begin`, an `until` line up with its corresponding `repeat`, an `else` line up with its corresponding `then`, etc.

- Indent the bodies of `label`, `const`, `type`, and `var` declarations and the bodies of `begin`, `for`, `while`, `repeat`, and `case` statements.

- Line up the `begin` and `end` statements of programs, procedures, and functions at the left margin with the heading.

These hints are illustrated in the following example:

```
type
  subint = 1..10;
  matrix = array[subint,subint] of real;
var
  a: matrix;
(* This procedure prints a matrix in *)
(* two-dimensional format.            *)
procedure printmatrix(var a: matrix);
var
  i, j: subint;
begin
  for i := 1 to 10 do
    begin
      for j := 1 to 10 do
        write(a[i,j]:7:2);
      writeln
    end
end;
```

Some computer centers have "pretty printing" programs that will do this formatting automatically for you. Ask your instructor if your computer center has such a program and if you may use it for the programming assignments in your class.

28 Expressive expressions are nicely nested.

In Pascal there are operator precedence rules that govern the order in which algebraic and boolean operations are done. Unparenthesized algebraic expressions are evaluated from left to right but multiplication and division are performed before addition and subtraction. Unparenthesized boolean expressions are also evaluated from left to right but **not**'s are applied before **and**'s, and **and**'s are applied before **or**'s.

You should learn these precedence rules and then choose to add extra parentheses to clarify the meaning of expressions that you write. Although parentheses may not be necessary, when an expression becomes complicated, it is helpful to use parentheses to avoid ambiguity and to improve readability.

For example, suppose you write the following statement

```
value := a * b / 2.0 * c;
```

which is interpreted by the computer as

```
value := ((a * b) / 2.0) * c;
```

Without the parentheses, someone reading your program may think that you meant

```
value := (a * b) / (2.0 * c);
```

If you clarify with parentheses, there is less chance of any confusion. As another example, consider

```
if not p and q or (a < b) then
```

which is logically equivalent to

```
if ((not p) and q) or (a < b) then
```

and not

```
if (not (p and q)) or (a < b) then
```

To clarify the meaning of a boolean expression, you may choose to use extra parentheses around subexpressions joined by **not**, **and**, and **or**.

Do not, however, use so many parentheses that they confuse the statement rather than clarify it. Here are three ways to write the same assignment statement:

1. `sum := a/b + c/d + e/f;`

2. `sum := (a/b) + (c/d) + (e/f);`

3. `sum := (((a/b) + (c/d)) + (e/f));`

Example 1 is clear, and 2 makes the operations perfectly clear, but 3 is overdone with too many parentheses.

If a boolean expression consists of a number of expressions joined by **and** and **or**, you may choose to introduce boolean variables and use them in place of the boolean subexpressions in the more complicated expression to clarify the statement.

29 Full stop to extra semicolons.

A semicolon is a statement separator, not part of a statement. **Begin** and **end** are not statements, but merely markers that designate the beginning and ending of Pascal statements. Thus, a semicolon must not be used after **begin** and is not needed before **end**.

An **if-then-else** statement includes the actions following **then** and **else**. Thus, a semicolon must not be used before **then** or **else**. For example, consider the following fragment, which prints the ith element of an array, if it is negative.

```
if (1 <= i) and (i <= n) then
    if a[i] < 0 then
        writeln('a[', i:1, '] = ', a[i]:2)
    else;
else
    writeln('i is outside the bounds of the array a.');
```

The semicolon after the first **else** is syntactically incorrect. The compiler is quite happy about the empty statement between the **else** and the semicolon, but a syntax error exists because the semicolon occurs immediately before the second **else**. As it is, the second **else** does not occur as part of any statement; it is a dangling **else**.

Now, if we remove the first **else** and the semicolon, the statement is syntactically correct, but the remaining **else** is associated with the second **if**, which is clearly not the original intention. If, instead, we remove only the semicolon (leaving an empty **else**), the statement is both syntactically and logically correct, but it is difficult to understand. To make this fragment both clear and correct, we need to bracket the inner **if** with **begin-end**, as follows:

```
(* This fragment prints the ith element *)
(* of an array a, if it is negative.    *)

if (1 <= i) and (i <= n) then
   begin
     if a[i] < 0 then
        writeln('a[', i:1, '] = ', a[i]:2)
   end
else
   writeln('i is outside the bounds of the array a.');
```

The **for** and **while** statements include the action following the **do**. If a semicolon is placed immediately after a **do**, the compiler sees an empty statement between the **do** and the semicolon. Consider the following fragment, which is supposed to print the n items of the array item in reverse order:

```
for i := n downto 1 do;
   writeln('item[', i:2, '] = ', item[i]:10);
```

The semicolon following the **do** is misplaced. The loop is executed n times, but nothing is printed within the loop. The semicolon following the **do** should be omitted.

Although extra semicolons should be avoided, note that semicolons are required after the program heading and before the declaration block, and also after the declaration block and before the statement block of your program, as shown below:

```
program example(input, output);
var
   r: real;
   b: boolean;
begin
   .
   .
end;
```

30 Unravel twisted logic.

> If it was so, it might be,
> and if it were so, it would be.
> But as it isn't, it ain't. That's logic.
>
> —Lewis Carroll

Sometimes, understanding logical expressions requires the skill of a puzzle-solving expert. Logical expressions are used with if-then statements, while and repeat loops, etc., and take on the values of true or false.

Computer science students are encouraged to take a course in formal logic, so that they can gain experience in dealing with logical expressions. Most colleges and universities offer an introductory course in logic (often through the Philosophy Department), or a course in discrete mathematics, in which formal logic is covered. Consult your college catalog for the logic course offered at your school.

In an introductory logic course, students learn to mind their "p's and q's" (so to speak). Consider the following example:

$$((\text{if } p \text{ then } q) \text{ and } p) \text{ therefore } q$$

This "conditional valid form" is known as "modus ponens" by logicians and is written in shorthand symbolic form as

$$(p => q) * p \therefore q$$

where

p stands for "p is true" (same for q)
=> stands for "implies"
* stands for "and"
∴ stands for "therefore."

For someone with no experience in symbolic logic, this looks pretty confusing. If you are confused, don't worry (your Pascal instructor is not going to quiz you on modus ponens). Nevertheless, as you proceed in your computer science career, experience with symbolic logic will be a real asset.

As a down-to-earth example of how to apply this logic, let's consider the weather. (Did you say whether?) If we let q mean "it's raining" and p mean "its cloudy," then by modus ponens, we can take the logical expression above to mean

If it's raining, then it's cloudy,
and it's raining;
therefore, it's cloudy.

At some time in your life you have, no doubt, been deluged with experiences of rain and dark clouds; therefore, you should realize that it is incorrect to say

If it's raining, then it's cloudy,
and it's cloudy;
therefore, it's raining.

This is an example of faulty logical reasoning, which would be expressed in symbolic logic as

((if p then q) and q) therefore p

Note the difference between this incorrect rule and the correct rule given above. Similarly, it is incorrect to say

If it's cloudy, then it's raining,
and it's cloudy;
therefore, it's raining.

Here the problem is that, although we applied the rule of logic correctly, we started from an incorrect assumption, namely: If it's cloudy, then it's raining.

If you are still under the weather about this example, then perhaps we have shed some light on why you should be interested in learning to apply symbolic logic to your programming problems. By completing a logic course, you can improve your programming skills (and perhaps even your expository writing, because logical thinking is important in exposition), and you will be better prepared for those math courses in which you will learn how to prove things.

Now, let's consider an example of how one logical expression may be transformed into a less confusing expression by using a law learned in logic. Suppose you are the landlord of a large student housing apartment complex. You are pretty "laidback" about having to collect late rent because you know that students sometimes have trouble paying the rent. Therefore, you have instituted a rule that you will not kick someone "out into the street" unless they fail to pay the rent for 2 months in a row.

Having decided to use modern technology to become a "1980s landlord," you buy a computer, so that you can computerize your rent accounting system. (Of course, your new machine has a Pascal compiler!) When you write your program, you declare the following variables:

```
var
    paidthismonth, paidlastmonth: boolean;
```

Now, to decide whether you should evict the tenant for failing to pay the rent, you write the following code fragment:

```
(* Decide whether or not to evict. *)
if not paidthismonth and not paidlastmonth then
    writeln('Throw him out on his tail!!!');
```

But perhaps the fragment would be easier to understand if you wrote it in the following way:

```
if not (paidthismonth or paidlastmonth) then
    writeln('Throw him out on his tail!!!');
```

Let's analyze why both of these logical expressions would work the same way. In logic, DeMorgan's Second Law gives equivalent valid forms, namely,

$$(\neg p * \neg q) \equiv \neg(p + q)$$

which means

> (not p) and (not q) is equivalent to not (p or q).

When we let p mean "paidthismonth is true" and q mean "paidlastmonth is true," then we can see that the two fragments above are equivalent. Be sure to convince yourself of this.

Some other equivalent logical expressions are

> (not p) or (not q) $\equiv$ not (p and q)
> (p or r) and (q or r) $\equiv$ (p and q) or r
> (p and r) or (q and r) $\equiv$ (p or q) and r.

You will be better able to understand the type of thinking illustrated in the example above after you have studied a course in logic. You will also have an easier time transforming hard-to-understand logical expressions when writing or debugging computer programs.

31 Is your code good reading matter?

Reading your code after putting it away for awhile is an excellent way to determine how well you are structuring and commenting your programs. In school you write programs within a 1 or 2 week period and then turn them in as complete assignments. In the "real world" you may work on a program and then have to put it away for several months to work on more pressing assignments. After the months pass, you will naturally have to spend some time reviewing your program, but your review time will be relatively painless if you have written structured, well-commented, and readable code.

Problems and Projects

1. Choose meaningful names and write declarations for variables that represent

    (a) A person's day, month, and year of birth.

    (b) A tape collection of rock, jazz, and classical music.

    (c) A Christmas card address list.

    (d) A furniture store inventory.

2. The program given in Proverb 26 lacks most of the comments that good programming style requires. Write comments for this program that aid in its understandability.

3. If p and q are both false and if r and s are both true, what is the value of each of the following expressions in Pascal?

    (a) p **or** q **or** r **and** **not** s.

    (b) **not** p **and** q **or** r **and** s.

    (c) p **or** r **and** s **or** **not** q **and** s.

    (d) (p = r) **or** **not** q.

4. Consider one of the programs you wrote several weeks or months ago. Is it as clear to you now as it was when you first wrote it? How does your programming style compare to the style suggested in this chapter? How can the readability and style of your program be improved?

5. Most people who buy a house need to borrow money for its purchase in the form of a mortgage. The money borrowed is repaid in equal monthly installments over a relatively long period of time, usually 20 or 30 years. What a prospective homeowner needs to know is how much the equal monthly payments will be. The formula for the amount A of the monthly installment is

$$A = P \times r \times (1 + r)^n / (1 + r)^n - 1$$

where P is the principal (the amount borrowed), r is the monthly interest rate (the annual interest rate/100/12), and n is the number of monthly payments (the number of years $\times$ 12). Write a program that computes the monthly installment for a principal of $100,000 over a period of 30 years with interest rates of 10, 10.5, 11, 11.5, 12, 12.5, and 13%. Make your program legible by including meaningful identifiers, descriptive comments, and appropriate indentation.

6. In Proverb 28 you read about the use of parentheses to clarify the meaning of expressions. State whether the following statements are true or false and explain why.

(a) The boolean expression

   not (p **and** q) **or** r

   is equivalent to

   not p **and** q **or** r.

(b) None of the parentheses in the expression

   not((x = y) **or** (y = z))

   can be omitted, without changing the validity or the meaning of the expression.

7. Write a Pascal program for the Bang-up Car Rental Company to analyze their car rentals. The program will read in the number of cars
   rented per day for a 1-year period; it will calculate their mean, variance, and standard deviation; and it will print these quantities with
   appropriate labels. The mean m is just the average of the numbers,
   that is,

$$m = \frac{\sum_1^n x_i}{n}$$

   The variance v is the average of the square of the deviations of the
   numbers from the mean, that is,

$$v = \frac{\sum_1^n (x_i - m)^2}{n}$$

   and the standard deviation σ is the square root of the variance,
   that is,

$$\sigma = \sqrt{v}$$

   Pay particular attention to your choice of variable names and your
   use of parentheses in this program. Have a friend read your program
   to see if he or she understands it.

8. Find out whether your computer center has a pretty printing program
   and, if it does, use it to pretty print the automated grading program
   you wrote in Chapter 2, Problem 8. Note any differences between the
   way the pretty printing program formatted your code and the way
   you wrote it. Which format do you prefer?

4
Robust
Programming

Industrial strength programs are sturdy, strongly constructed, and designed for vigorous use. This chapter covers program generalization, constant declaration, input preparation, variable initialization, real number manipulation, graceful degradation, error preparation, and program (pardon us) "portabilitation." Apply these proverbs to your software engineering efforts to construct tough and rugged programs.

Real-world applications are where the proverbs on robust programming realize their significance. Today, computers are used for critical applications, such as life-support systems, transportation systems, and defense-related systems. The robustness of the software used in such applications is crucial for the safety of those involved. An unrecognized input error, an uninitialized variable, or a mishandled real number can lead to disaster! Though you may not be working on applications of such a critical nature immediately, a thorough understanding of the proverbs in this chapter will help you to produce industrial strength programs.

32 A general program is a major saving.

When writing a program to solve some specific problem, write it as generally as possible so that it can be used over again to solve similar problems. Consider the following case in point. Al Gorithm, a high school math teacher, has written a program to calculate the average scores of the students on a test in his algebra class. There are 30 students in the class, so he wrote the following code:

```
(* This program computes the average score *)
(* on the first test of the 30 students in *)
(* Algebra I.                               *)
program computeaverage(input, output);
var
    totalscore: 0..100;
    avgscore: real;
    i: 1..30;
    studentscore: array[1..30] of 0..100;
begin
    studentscore[1]  := 85;
    studentscore[2]  := 70;
    studentscore[3]  := 93;

        .

        .

    studentscore[30] := 68;

    totalscore := 0;
    for i := 1 to 30 do
        totalscore := totalscore + studentscore[i];
    avgscore := totalscore / 30;

    writeln('Student Scores ');
    for i := 1 to 30 do
        writeln(studentscore[i]:14);
    writeln('Average score = ', avgscore:5:2)
end.
```

As it is written, Al can only use this piece of code once for the specific scores encoded for the 30 students in the class. Instead, he should have read in the scores of the students at the terminal. Even after making this change, his program is too restrictive. After the first exam, nine students dropped Al's class because they thought his tests were too hard. After the second exam, he realized that his program would not work any longer because he only had 21 scores to average instead of 30. Al should have read in the number of students rather than "hard-wire" the number throughout the code. He rewrote his program more generally so that it could be used for his classes in the future. Notice that he declared the constant maxclassize, which, along with the variable classize, makes it easy to accomodate a larger class.

```pascal
(* This program reads in an arbitrary number  *)
(* of student scores and computes the average *)
(* score of the class.                        *)
program computeaverage(input, output);
const
  maxclassize = 30;
var
  totalscore: 0..maxint;
  avgscore: real;
  i, classize: 1..maxclassize;
  studentscore: array[1..maxclassize] of 0..100;
begin
  writeln('Input the class size');
  readln(classize);
  writeln('Input the student scores, one per line');
  for i := 1 to classize do
    readln(studentscore[i]);

  totalscore := 0;
  for i := 1 to classize do
    totalscore := totalscore + studentscore[i];
  avgscore := totalscore / classize;

  writeln('Student Scores ');
  for i := 1 to classize do
    writeln(studentscore[i]:14);
  writeln;
  writeln('Average score = ', avgscore:5:2)
end.
```

When the size of the class changes because someone adds or drops it or a new term starts, he simply reads in a new value of `classize`, reads in the students' scores, and the class average is computed. As this example shows, it's best to avoid the tendency to write overly restricted code. Remember, a general program is a major saving.

A GENERAL PROGRAMMING

33 Declare your constants, because you may need to change them.

Any constant that (1) is used frequently within a program, (2) could possibly be changed in future versions of the program, or (3) is important in understanding a part of the logic of a program should be defined symbolically in a **const** declaration.

In the preceding example, Al declared `maxclassize` as a constant. The maximum class size is referred to several times in the declarations, and although it is currently set at 30, this could very well change in the future. Therefore, it is appropriate that `maxclassize` be declared as a constant.

Let's suppose now that Al wants to compute the area and circum-ference of a circle and print the results to three decimal places. Having learned from his previous experience, he now writes the following code:

```
(* This program computes the area    *)
(* and circumference of a circle of *)
(* given radius.                     *)

program circle(input, output);
const
   pi = 3.14159;
   fieldwidth = 7;
   decimalplaces = 3;
var
   radius, area, circum: real;
begin
   writeln('Input the radius.');
   readln(radius);

   area := pi * sqr(radius);
   circum := 2 * pi * radius;

   writeln('For a circle of radius ',
           radius:fieldwidth:decimalplaces);
   writeln('the area is ',
           area:fieldwidth:decimalplaces);
   writeln('the circumference is ',
           circum:fieldwidth:decimalplaces)
end.
```

Because pi is a universal constant used in the formulas for comput-ing the area and circumference of a circle and because the field width and the number of decimal places are used several times in the writeln statements and could be changed in future versions of the program, they should be declared as constants.

To change the number of decimal places, for example, Al can simply change the constant decimalplaces. This results in a change throughout the entire program wherever the constant decimalplaces is referenced.

34 On input, be ready for anything.

Subrange and enumeration types are very helpful to use in the internal parts of your program because they add to its clarity and they aid the compiler in error checking. But enumeration types cannot be used for input or output, and subrange types should not be used for input, particularly if the program will be used by others.

A user can become very aggravated if he or she accidentally types the letter "y" instead of the number "6" and causes the program to terminate in the middle of a long data entry session. In the input section of a program that is written for other users, it's best to use the full range of integers or characters, so that if the user accidentally types the wrong character, the entire program won't blow up[1] with a message like

```
Value out of range
```

For example, when reading in a date in the form *mm/dd/yy*, instead of writing

```
(* This fragment reads in a date in the form    *)
(* mm/dd/yy, where the month, day, and year are *)
(* integers, each in a restricted subrange.     *)
```

```
type
   month = 1..12;
   day   = 1..31;
   year  = 0..99;
var
   m: month;
   d: day;
   y: year;
   slash: char;
begin
   readln(m, slash, d, slash, y);
   .
   .
   .
```

---

[1] Blow up—terminate with an error message from the operating system.

and letting the program abort if the user hits the wrong key, it would be better to use the following method, because it allows the user to input characters other than digits for m, d, and y. The program itself rejects invalid data rather than terminating when a nondigit is entered.

```
(* This fragment reads in a date in the form      *)
(* mm/dd/yy, where the month, day, and year are    *)
(* represented as character strings.  It converts *)
(* these strings to integers and checks that the   *)
(* integers fall in the proper ranges for months,  *)
(* days, and years.                                *)
type
   subint = 0..maxint;
   astring = array[1..2] of char;
var
   slash: char;
   ms, ds, ys: astring;
   m, d, y: subint;
   valid: boolean;

procedure readstring(var s: astring);
var
   i: 1..2;
begin
   for i := 1 to 2 do
      read(s[i])
end;

(* This function converts a string *)
(* to an integer.                  *)
function int(s: astring): subint;
begin
   int := (ord(s[1])-ord('0'))*10 + ord(s[2])-ord('0')
end;
   .
   .
   .
```

```
  .
  .
  .
begin
  writeln('Input the month, day, and year ',
          'in the format mm/dd/yy');
  readstring(ms);
  read(slash);
  readstring(ds);
  read(slash);
  readstring(ys);
  readln;

  (* Convert the month from character to integer form *)
  (* and check that it is valid.                      *)
  valid := false;
  while not valid do
    begin
      if (ms[1] in ['0'..'9']) and
         (ms[2] in ['0'..'9']) then
        begin
          m := int(ms);
          if m in [1..12] then
            valid := true
        end;
      if not valid then
        begin
          writeln(ms[1], ms[2], ' is not a valid month.',
                  'Please input the month again.');
          readstring(ms);
          readln
        end
    end;

  (* Convert the day from character to integer form *)
  (* and check that it is valid.                    *)
  valid := false;
```

```
while not valid do
  begin
    if (ds[1] in ['0'..'9']) and
       (ds[2] in ['0'..'9']) then
      begin
        d := int(ds);
        if d in [1..31] then
          valid := true
      end;
    if not valid then
      begin
        writeln(ds[1], ds[2], ' is not a valid day.',
                'Please input the day again.');
        readstring(ds);
        readln
      end
  end;
(* Convert the year from character to integer form  *)
(* and check that it is valid.                      *)
valid := false;
while not valid do
  begin
    if (ys[1] in ['0'..'9']) and
       (ys[2] in ['0'..'9']) then
      begin
        y := int(ys);
        if y in [0..99] then
          valid := true
      end;
    if not valid then
      begin
        writeln(ys[1], ys[2], ' is not a valid year.',
                'Please input the year again.');
        readstring(ys);
        readln
      end
  end;
```

35 If you don't say where you're starting from, you won't get where you're going.

To have any hope of getting the correct results from your program, you must initialize each variable before you use it. That is, you must assign a value to the variable before you take a value out of it. Remember, a variable declaration only sets up a storage location for a variable—it doesn't put a value there. You must give the variable a value in an assignment statement or a read statement. Otherwise, the "garbage" that was left in the variable by you or some other user will be used in your calculation.

For example, Romeo kept his very private address list on the computer. He wrote the following procedure to read the names of his friends into strings of characters:

```
type
   astring = array[1..30] of char;

procedure readstring(var name: astring);
var
   i: 0..30;
begin
   i := 0;
   while not eoln and (i < 30) do
      begin
         i := i + 1;
         read(name[i])
      end;
   readln
end;
```

Notice that he correctly initialized the local variable i within the procedure. But, nevertheless, Juliet was surprised to receive a birthday card addressed to Juliet*?%%xfvv>.p2df:*/=ggtb$. Because Juliet's name has less than 30 characters, the rest of the components in the array had garbage in them. (Romeo was very lucky that it was meaningless garbage rather than part of some other girl friend's name.)

Romeo had forgotten to initialize the components explicitly with something else. He might have initialized the array, for example, with blanks and overwritten the blanks with the characters read in.

```
procedure readstring(var name: astring);
var
   i: 0..30;
begin
   for i := 1 to 30 do
     name[i] := ' ';
   i := 0;
   while not eoln and (i < 30) do
     begin
       i := i + 1;
       read(name[i])
     end;
   readln
end;
```

Here's another case in point. Ebenezer Scrooge wanted to calculate how much extra profit he had made on his investments by insisting on being paid compound interest rather than simple interest (at two points over the prime, of course). Thus, he wrote the following function to compute his extra profit:

```
type
   posint = 1..50;
   primearray = array[posint] of real;

function extraprofit(years: posint; principal: real;
                     var prime: primearray): real;
var
   i: posint;
   simple, compound: real;
begin
   for i := 1 to years do
      begin
         simple := simple + prime[i] + 0.02;
         compound := compound * (prime[i] + 1.02)
      end;
   compound := compound - 1.0;
   extraprofit := (compound - simple) * principal
end;
```

Unfortunately, Scrooge got the wrong answers because he forgot to initialize simple and compound. The final results were unpredictable and very different from what he expected. The ghost of Jacob Marley suggested that the initialization statements

```
simple := 0.0;
compound := 1.0;
```

be inserted between the **begin** and **for** i lines in the function. Scrooge rewrote the function so that the two variables were initialized correctly, and then the program provided him with the correct results.

```
function extraprofit(years: posint; principal: real;
                     var prime: primearray): real;
var
  i: posint;
  simple, compound: real;
begin
  simple := 0.0;
  compound := 1.0;
  for i := 1 to years do
    begin
      simple := simple + prime[i] + 0.02;
      compound := compound * (prime[i] + 1.02)
    end;
  compound := compound - 1.0;
  extraprofit := (compound - simple) * principal
end;
```

36 Reinitialization bears repeating.

Besides ensuring that you have initialized all variables before use, you must also make sure that variables in inner loops are properly reinitialized between successive uses. If you do not reinitialize at just the right point in a nested loop, the results that you compute will be meaningless.

For example, the owners of the Pluperfect Software Company (a company owned and operated by "has beens") need to know how many of each of their programs have been sold each month. They keep a sales matrix dailysales that gives, for each program and each day of the month, the number sold on that day. The rows of the matrix correspond to the different programs, a through k, and the columns correspond to the days of the month, 1 through 31. In creating the matrix dailysales, they have remembered the preceding proverb and properly initialized the matrix, so that for months with fewer than 31 days and for days, such as holidays, on which no programs are sold, there is a zero in the appropriate position of the matrix. Now they need a procedure that computes the monthly sales for each program.

```
type
   nonnegint = 0..maxint;
   day = 1..31;
   prog = 'a'..'k';
   salesmatrix = array[prog,day] of nonnegint;
   salesvector = array[prog] of nonnegint;

(* This procedure finds the monthly sales for each *)
(* of several software programs, as the sum of     *)
(* daily sales.                                     *)

procedure computcmonthlysales(dailysales: salesmatrix;
                            var monthlysales: salesvector);
var
   i: prog;
   j: day;
   subtotal: nonnegint;
begin
   subtotal := 0;
   for i := 'a' to 'k' do
      begin
         for j := 1 to 31 do
            subtotal := subtotal + dailysales[i,j];
         monthlysales[i] := subtotal
      end
end;
```

Although subtotal is initialized in the procedure, it is not properly reinitialized in the loop. The monthly sales for program a will be correct, but the monthly sales for the rest of the programs will not. As computed by this procedure, the monthly sales for program b will include the monthly sales for program a, the monthly sales for program c will include the monthly sales for programs a and b, etc. The monthly sales for program k will be the total sales of all the programs, not just the sales of program k. They revise their procedure so that subtotal is reinitialized each time through the loop.

```
(* This procedure finds the monthly sales for each    *)
(* of several software programs, as the sum of their *)
(* daily sales.                                        *)

procedure computemonthlysales(dailysales: salesmatrix;
                             var monthlysales: salesvector);
var
   i: prog;
   j: day;
   subtotal: nonnegint;
begin
   for i := 'a' to 'k' do
     begin
       subtotal := 0;
       for j := 1 to 31 do
         subtotal := subtotal + dailysales[i,j];
       monthlysales[i] := subtotal
     end
end;
```

37 Careless use of real numbers can lead to imaginary results.

Real numbers that have an infinite decimal representation cannot be stored exactly in a computer—only a finite number of digits can be stored. This introduces small but distinct truncation errors. If computations are performed using these truncated values, the results will also be in error. Small errors in the representation can accumulate to produce large errors in the computed results.

For example, the Chatterbox Phone Company needs to know approximately how many phone calls are made each day in total. The company has a computer that is accurate to only six decimal places. (Computers are usually more accurate, but accuracy to six decimal places suffices for illustration purposes.) The computer truncates digits that don't fit. The total number of calls made each day is found by adding together the number of calls made from each telephone number. Because the company has many customers who chatter a lot, the total number of calls is very large, much larger than maxint.[2] Thus, the real number representation appears to be appropriate. One of the company's programmers writes

```
type
   subint = 1..maxcust;
   subint1 = 0..maxcustplus1;
   callsarray = array[subint] of real;

(* This function finds the total number of calls *)
(* for all telephone numbers.                    *)
function totalcalls(numcustomers: subint1;
            var numcalls: callsarray): real;
var
   total: real;
   i: subint1;
begin
   total := 0.0;
   i := 1;
   while i <= numcustomers do
      begin
         total := total + numcalls[i];
         i := i + 1
      end;
   totalcalls := total
end;
```

When the programmer runs the program, all goes well for the first few hundred thousand telephone numbers. However, when the total number of calls is, say, 1,000,000 and one more call is added in, the result

---

[2]Maxint—the maximum allowable integer value. Its exact value depends on the particular computer.

(which is 1,000,001) is truncated to 1,000,000. The effect of adding in 1 has been lost. Even if the next 1,000,000 customers have made one call each, the total will still be 1,000,000 after adding them all in. Note that the effect of truncation is not just to introduce a small error in the result, but it can render the result completely meaningless.

Here is another typical example. The Bang-Up Car Rental Company wanted to know how many miles had been driven by people who paid with the Bang-Up credit card. Joe wrote

```
type
   rec = record
            outmileage, inmileage: real;
            card: (bangup, ... );
            .

            .
         end;
   arrayofrec = array[1..maxrentals] of rec;

(* This function computes the total miles driven     *)
(* by people who paid with the Bang-Up credit card.  *)

function totalmileage(numrentals: nonnegint;
                  var rentalrecs: arrayofrec): real;
var
   outtotal, intotal: real;
   i: nonnegint;
begin
   outtotal := 0.0;
   intotal := 0.0;
   for i := 1 to numrentals do
      if rentalrecs[i].card = bangup then
        begin
           outtotal := outtotal+rentalrecs[i].outmileage;
           intotal := intotal+rentalrecs[i].inmileage
        end;
   totalmileage := intotal - outtotal
end;
```

The results were all wrong. Can you explain why? The problem is that Joe's function totals up all of the outmileage's and all of the inmileage's, producing two rather large numbers. If these two numbers were represented entirely accurately, their difference would indeed be the required Bang-Up mileage. But the computation of the two totals introduces truncation errors, errors that are small relative to each total but large relative to the much smaller difference between them. It would have been better to calculate the difference for each car individually and then sum these differences to produce the total.

The cause of the difficulty is basically the same in both of these examples. A real number can be represented by the computer with a possible error due to truncation that is proportional to the magnitude of the number. The size of this truncation error is less than the number times 10^{-6} for almost all computers. (On some computers real numbers can be represented with a truncation error of as little as the number times 10^{-15}.)

When large numbers are involved, a small relative error can be quite a large absolute error.[3] In particular, when adding or subtracting, the size of the truncation error is determined by the largest number (in absolute magnitude) involved. Thus, when a small number is added to a very large number, the absolute size of the error can be as large as the small number. Similarly, when two nearly equal large numbers are subtracted,

---

[3]The absolute error is the actual error, whereas the relative error is the ratio of the absolute error to the data value. For a data value of, say, 10^{10} an absolute error of 10^4 would be a relative error of 10^{-6}.

the absolute error in the result can be quite small relative to the original numbers but can still be large compared with the small result. Thus, when using real numbers, try to arrange your program so that the numbers you add and subtract, and also the results, are not very different in size.

The problem is somewhat different for multiplication and division of real numbers (or integers, for that matter). When multiplying or dividing two very large or very small numbers, be careful that you don't exceed the range of the machine. For real numbers this is usually not a problem unless your program has gone wrong, because their range is very large. The range of integers, on the other hand, is quite limited, so be careful not to exceed that range. If there's any doubt, use a real number instead.

You must also be careful when using real numbers in conditions in loops and `if-then-else` statements. Never test for exact equality of real numbers but, rather, test only for approximate equality. Instead of testing

```
if  x = y  then
```

it is better to test

```
if abs(x - y) < epsilon then
```

where `epsilon` is some small tolerable error, such as 0.0001. For example, if

$$x = 0.33330000 \quad \text{and} \quad y = 0.33333334$$

and you only require accuracy to four decimal places, then x and y are both reasonable approximations to one-third and you may consider them to be equal. If x and y can range widely in magnitude, it might be better to write

```
if abs(x - y) < epsilon * (abs(x) + abs(y)) then
```

thus allowing your measure of approximate equality to change in size as x and y change in size.

Error, as it pertains to the accuracy of real numbers on a computer, is an important topic of discussion in numerical analysis. For the student who plans to program numerical applications, a course in numerical analysis is a must. If you take the course from an instructor who emphasizes use of the computer as a numerical tool, then you will study, in depth, the accuracy of real numbers in computations.

38 When the going gets tough, tough programs get graceful degradation.

As you become a more experienced programmer, the complexity of your programs will increase, and as a result, there will be many more places in your code where things can go wrong. Nevertheless, as a programmer, you should always be in charge and maintain control of the execution of your program. Rather than letting your program blow up when faced with the unexpected, prepare your program so that it will degrade gracefully when the unexpected occurs.

By graceful degradation, we mean that your program, instead of blowing up, degrades by producing a less complete result than what you intended. A program that does less than the ideal calculation, but nevertheless does something useful, is better than a program that ends abnormally and tells you nothing more than that it ended abnormally.

To provide for graceful degradation, take steps to prevent the computer from gaining control and spontaneously aborting your program when run-time errors occur. Common run-time errors include

- Values of array subscripts or **case** selectors that go out of range.

- Functions that become undefined when inappropriate values of the arguments are given, such as sqrt(x) for x < 0, or pred(day) for day = sun, or succ(day) for day = sat, when day is a variable of type (sun,mon,tue,wed,thu,fri,sat).

- Division by zero.

Provide meaningful error messages in your program and reassign variables that have inappropriate values with values that will allow the program to continue. Get as much information as possible out of each program run.

If, for example, you find that a negative value occurs in computing the value of your venture capital investments, you might set the value to zero and allow the program to continue.

```pascal
type
  posint = 1..numcompanies;
  nonnegint = 0..maxshares;
  quotationarray = array[posint] of real;
  numberarray = array[posint] of nonnegint;

(* This function computes the total value of       *)
(* investments by multiplying the share quotation  *)
(* by the number of shares for each investment     *)
(* and summing up these results.  Invalid values   *)
(* for the share quotations or the number of       *)
(* shares are set to 0.                            *)

function totalvalue(var sharequotation: quotationarray;
                    var numberofshares: numberarray): real;
var
  i: posint;
  total: real;
begin
  total := 0;
  for i := 1 to numcompanies do
    if sharequotation[i] < 0 then
      begin
        writeln('The share quote for company ', i:4,
                ' is incorrect.  The quote is negative: ',
                sharequotation[i]:5:2);
        writeln('The value will be set to 0.');
        value[i] :=  0
      end
```

```
else if numberofshares[i] < 0 then
  begin
    writeln('The number of shares for company ', i:4,
            ' in the portfolio is incorrect. ',
            ' The number is negative: ',
            numberofshares[i]:4);
    writeln('The value will be set to 0.');
    value[i] := 0
  end
else
  begin
    value[i] := sharequotation[i]*numberofshares[i];
    total := total + value[i]
  end;
  totalvalue := total
end;
```

Plan for graceful degradation by providing some alternative action whenever something might go wrong, and print a statement that describes the action you took. The thing to remember is that if your program can't do the ideal calculation, it should still do something useful. The results you get may not all that you intended, but at least something is better than nothing.

39 Raise a flag to conquer errors.

Before using the values returned by a procedure or function, it's a good idea to check whether the values computed are in error. To check whether a procedure or function is working properly, you can include an error flag among its parameters. In this way, you are installing a "red light" that will go on whenever your black box fails to operate properly.

Let's consider an example. Because Pascal does not have a built-in power function, you cannot compute y^x directly. Instead, you have to write your own function or procedure, using the logarithm and exponential functions provided by Pascal and the fact that $y^x = e^{x \ln y}$. Now y^x

and $\ln y$ are real valued functions only if $y > 0$, and in Pascal, $\ln y$ is a
real valued function. Therefore, you should include an error flag in the
procedure that you write to cover the possibility that $y \le 0$.

```
(* This procedure finds the xth power of y and  *)
(* returns it in ytothex.  If y is less than or *)
(* equal to 0, it sets the error flag to true.  *)
procedure findpower(y, x: real;
             var ytothex: real; var errorflag: boolean);
begin
  if y <= 0 then
    errorflag := true
  else
    begin
      ytothex := exp(x * ln(y));
      errorflag := false
    end
end; (* Procedure findpower *)
```

In the program that calls this procedure, the programmer would test
the error flag after calling findpower, as follows:

```
begin
  writeln('To find the ath power of b, ');
  writeln('first enter the base b.');
  readln(b);

  writeln('Now enter the exponent a.');
  readln(a);

  findpower(b, a, btothea, errorflag);

  if errorflag then
    writeln('Error!!!  The base b is ', b:7:2,
            ', which is less than or equal to 0.');
  else
    writeln(b:7:2, ' to the ', a:7:2, 'th power is ',
            btothea:7:2)
end;
```

Of course, there might be more than one possible kind of error. It would then be appropriate to use an enumeration type to represent the error flag. For example, the Bang-up Car Rental Company must compute a charge based on mileage, and there are several possible errors in recording the mileage and the number of days a car was rented. Thus, their procedure might look like

```
type
    errors =
         (ok,nodays,noinmileage,nooutmileage,checkmileage);
    rentalrec = record
                    inmileage, outmileage: real;
                    days: integer
               end;
(* This proccduro computes a charge for car rental *)
(* based on mileage.  A flag is used to signal an   *)
(* error in the mileage which occurs in the rental  *)
(* record.                                          *)
procedure computecharge(r: rentalrec;
                 var charge: real; var errorflag: errors);
begin
    if r.days = 0 then
       errorflag := nodays
    if r.outmileage = 0.0 then
       errorflag := nooutmileage
    else if r.inmileage = 0.0 then
       errorflag := noinmileage
    else if (r.inmileage - r.outmileage < 0.0) or
       ((r.inmileage - r.outmileage)/r.days > 1000.0) then
       errorflag := checkmileage
    else
       begin
          errorflag := ok;
          charge := ...
       end
end;
```

Skillful use of error flags can make your program more robust. But excessive numbers of error flags will make your program too complex, and it will be very difficult to test all of the error conditions properly. You should certainly use error flags, but try to keep them simple.

40 Portable programs go further.

Portable programs are programs that can be transferred to different machines or compilers with a minimum of modification. In the real world, programs are written to run on many different machines because they are sold or traded; therefore, portability is important. Also, when new machines are installed, portable programs need less rewriting than do nonportable programs.

If you're writing a program that may be run on different machines with different compilers, use the standard version of the language. Some implementations of Pascal have special capabilities for handling strings. When you're using such an implementation, string processing may be much easier. But if you use a different implementation, your program may not work at all and may have to be rewritten substantially.

When choosing identifiers, make your programs portable by ensuring that the first eight characters of each identifier are different from the first eight characters of every other identifier. Nearly all implementations of

Pascal use at least the first eight characters to distinguish one identifier from another. If you use the declaration

```
var
    positionx, positiony: real;
```

in a program that is run on a compiler that accepts only the first eight characters as significant, then the two identifiers would be regarded as the same, resulting in a compilation error. Think how embarrassing it would be if your fully debugged Pascal program did not even compile on the new machine. If you always make sure that no two identifiers have the same first eight characters, then you will have less trouble when moving your code from machine to machine.

If a particular piece of code is system dependent (i.e., if it depends on a feature of your particular computing system), organize your program so that this system-dependent information is easy to locate and change. Don't bury these details in the depths of your program so that someone must painstakingly search for them. Make sure that you clearly comment and document this system-dependent code.

Suppose, for example, you are writing a program that requires as data the number of terminals in a particular time-sharing system network. Instead of assigning the number of terminals in statements throughout your code, use a **const** declaration at the top of your code, write a meaningful comment to indicate the use of this system-dependent part of the code, and use the constant in your code when referring to the number of terminals. For example,

```
(* This value represents the number *)
(* of terminals on the machine.      *)
(* You must change the declaration    *)
(* if the number available at your    *)
(* installation is different.          *)
const
    terminals = 10;
```

If the number of terminals changes often, then it might be even better to have terminals read in at the terminal.

You should also localize read and write statements in subprograms. Input and output are often the most system-dependent parts of a program. It is more efficient to put read and write statements all in one place than to have them scattered throughout a large program. The best way to do this is to have special procedures just for input and output. The next chapter offers advice for designing the input and output portions of your programs.

Problems and Projects

1. Write a procedure to solve a quadratic equation $ax^2 + bx + c = 0$, using the quadratic formula

$$x = \frac{-b \pm \sqrt{b^2 - 4ac}}{2a}$$

Your procedure should handle the regular cases, as well as the following special cases.

(a) A double root: $b^2 - 4ac = 0$.

(b) Complex roots: $b^2 - 4ac < 0$.

(c) A nonquadratic equation: $a = 0$.

(d) An illegal equation: $a = 0,\ b = 0$.

Make your program robust!

2. Write a program for Phyllis (see Proverb 19) to compute the average weights and heights of her clients. Make your program validate input to ensure that

(a) All weights are in the range 80 to 300 and all heights are in the range 4 to 8. Do not use a client in the calculations if his or her weight or height is outside the specified range.

(b) There is at least one client with a valid weight and height. If not, print an error message that there is no such client.

3. Write a Pascal program to compute the interest on money deposited in a savings account when the interest is compounded annually, quarterly, monthly, and daily. The formula you need to compute compound interest is

$$A = P \times (1 + \frac{r}{m})^{m \times n}$$

where A is the amount at the end of n years, P is the principal, r is the annual interest rate in decimal form, n is the number of years, and m is the number of times per year that the interest is compounded. Assume that there are 365 days per year and that all the principal is deposited at the beginning of the first year. Let the program user enter the interest rate and the principal.

4. Replay Magazine, the magazine for VCR owners, needs a program to generate mailing labels. The input will be in the following format:

    > last name, first name, middle initial, age, sex,
    > street number, street name, city, state,
    > zip code, expiration date

    where the expiration date is the month and year the subscription expires. Write a program to output a three-line mailing label in the following format:

    > first name   middle initial   last name
    > street number   street name
    > city,   state   zip code

    if and only if the expiration date is after the current date. Use strings of characters (rather than subrange types) for input, so that your program doesn't blow up if the user mistypes a character. Also, remember to initialize your strings to blanks. Don't make the same mistake as Romeo!

5. The military, secret service, and other agencies use computers to generate messages in encrypted form and also to analyze such cryptograms. One method of encryption uses character substitution. In this method, each character of the original text is replaced with a substitute. For example, if we have the correspondence

character: A B C D E F G H I J K L M N O P Q R S T U V W X Y Z
substitute: X H E L V R N A P W T Z G B J M U D Q Y K S O I F C

and the message we wish to send is

THEMARTIANSAREINVADINGTHISPLANET

then the encrypted message will be

YAVGXDYPXBQXDVPBSXLPBNYAPQMZXBVY

Write a program that implements this substitution method and that can be used either for encryption or for decryption. Make your program general and portable. It should be capable of handling text that contains characters other than letters of the alphabet and should not depend on the character/integer correspondence for your particular computer.

6. Write a Pascal program to process the weekly payroll of Ali Baba. Each week the employees turn in time cards that contain the following information: employee's name (at most 30 characters), social security number (9 digits), hourly pay rate ($xx.xx$), number of exemptions (0 to 19), health insurance code (1,2,3,4), and hours worked this week. Using this information, your program will compute the employee's

(a) Gross pay, which consists of regular pay for the first 40 hr and time-and-a-half for overtime, up to a maximum of 60 hr per week.

(b) Deductions, which include:
Federal income tax, computed as 20% of taxable income.
State income tax, computed as 10% of taxable income.
Social security tax, computed as 7% of gross pay.
Health insurance, which is coded as follows:
1 No coverage.
2 Employee coverage ($5 per week).
3 Employee and one family member ($12.50 per week).
4 Employee and two+ family members ($25 per week).

(c) Net pay, which is the gross pay less all deductions.

Your program will produce a monthly statement in a legible format with each item clearly labeled for each employee. It will also produce a paycheck. Your program must be capable of handling an arbitrary number of "employees" and should perform reasonable operations for all input data, no matter how meaningless. For example, what if an employee has worked more than 60 hr? What if taxable pay is negative? What if deductions exceed net pay? Be careful to check these and similar situations and take some appropriate action. Remember, tough programs degrade gracefully. You'll encounter this program again in Chapter 9, Problem 5, and in Chapter 11, Problem 1.

7. As we've discussed in Proverb 37, real numbers are stored in a computer in approximate form, and computation with real numbers introduces further inaccuracies. Write a driver program for the Chatterbox Phone Company's function totalcalls, and run the program on your computer. Did you get the results that you expected? Try increasingly large numbers until inaccuracies arise. What conclusions do you draw from this experiment?

8. Write a program to make airline seat assignments. Your program will assign seats on a first-come-first-served basis. The input will consist of a customer's name and a request, of the form

    > first class/coach
    > smoking/nonsmoking/don't care
    > window/aisle/don't care.

The program will display the seat pattern, with a U marking the unassigned seats that meet the requested conditions. For example, the unassigned first-class, nonsmoking, window seats might be displayed as follows:

	A	B	C	D	E	F	G	H	I	J	K
1	U										U
2	U										U
3	U										U
4											
.											
.											

The program will then prompt the airline clerk for a seat. After the airline clerk types in a row and seat, the program will update the display of available seats. If the clerk mistakenly types in a seat that is already assigned, then the program should say that the seat is occupied and ask for another choice. For each request, print the name of the customer and a message indicating whether or not his or her reservation is confirmed. This sequence continues until all of the seats are assigned or the clerk signals that the program should end. Apply the proverbs in this chapter to make your program robust!

9. If possible, try transporting a program that you wrote on one machine to another machine with a different Pascal compiler. Does your program still run? What changes did you have to make? How could you have made your program more portable?

5
Interactive
Programming

Only a few years ago, interacting with a computer required the use of cards; programmers could usually be identified in a crowd by the large boxes of cards they carried in their arms (or sometimes in shopping carts). These days, however, nearly everyone is using terminals or stand-alone microcomputers, if not for programming or data processing, then for relatively simple tasks such as getting money out of a bank. Today, people who don't even know a `while` loop from a ring on their finger are using computers. As a result, many additional demands are now made on the people who program these machines.

In this chapter you will read about ways of "dummy-proofing" your programs and making them "user friendly." This includes ways of accepting input into your programs and preparing for input errors and ways of presenting output in a fashion that can be easily read. It's time now to learn the ins and outs of interactive Pascal programming.

41 Reading problems? Read the manual.

When running programs interactively at a terminal, you may encounter some special problems in reading from the standard input file or writing to the standard output file. These "standard" files, when connected to a terminal, are handled differently by different systems.

On some systems, you should write (as you might have expected)

```
writeln('Enter the first character.');
readln(ch);
```

This will work on systems in which the read issues a prompt character to the user and waits for him or her to type. (Remember readln(ch) is defined to mean read(ch); readln.) However, there are some systems (particularly those derived from Professor Wirth's original implementation) on which this will not work. The effect may be that the user gets the prompt and must type before the message is printed. Such systems operate on the basis that it is the readln that issues the prompt character and solicits input. Thus, the appropriate sequence is

```
writeln('Enter the first character.');
readln;
read(ch);
```

When you construct a loop to read a string of characters, there are corresponding differences. For the first kind of system, you might write

```
writeln('Enter the first character.');
while not eof do
  begin
    readln(ch);
    process(ch);
    writeln('Enter the next character.')
  end;
```

For the second kind of system, the sequence would look like

```
writeln('Enter the first character.');
readln;
while not eof do
  begin
    read(ch);
    process(ch);
    writeln('Enter the next character.');
    readln
  end;
```

Of course, there may be computer systems for which yet other alternatives are required. You will have to read the manual for your system and follow the instructions given there.

42 Make your programs user friendly.

As programmers, we create tools that are used by other people. Our programs are often designed to solve problems for others or to help others do a particular task in a more efficient manner. For example, we may be involved in writing a customized word processing program for a small company or the grade report program for a major university. When writing programs for others, we must make them both easy to use and dummy proof.

Nearly all of the programs we write have potential for use by other people. Although we may initially think that no one else will ever use the programs that we write as projects for school or for ourselves, we should prepare the programs so that they can be used by others should someone want to use them in the future. You will be surprised how little you remember about how to use a program you yourself wrote a year ago. It is, therefore, a good idea to think of the user, particularly when designing the input and output portions of a program.

Computer professionals who recognize the importance of remembering the user write user-friendly programs. These programs feature easy-to-understand user prompts, accessible directions for proper use of the code, and logic to handle the inevitable mistakes of the human user. Many people who use computers know little or nothing about programming, so they must depend on the programmer to write code that is easy to use and fail-safe.

When writing interactive programs, you should provide meaningful prompts to inform the user of what to type next. "Help" options should be included to provide "on-line" documentation to remind the user of the method for running the program. You may wish to provide what one creative instructor calls an "oops key," a key that, when pressed, allows the user to correct an error or start over. Furthermore, output should be clearly labeled, so that all information provided by the program is both meaningful and useful. Don't miss the helpful hints for designing the input portions of your program in Proverbs 42 and 43 and the output portions of your program in Proverb 45.

As a programmer for Compubanker Software Company, you are asked to write a program to help a computer illiterate maintain his or her banking information on a home computer. Because the user knows nothing about programming and little about using programs, it is

particularly important that you add on-line help options that give simple instructions on what to do next when he or she requests help. For example, when the time comes for the user to enter checks into the computer, a procedure like the following might be useful.

```
procedure helpwithchecks;
begin
  writeln('To enter your checks for the month,');
  writeln('after each prompt, enter');
  writeln;
  writeln('check, checknumber, value<ret>');
  writeln;
  writeln('For example, if you wanted to enter ');
  writeln('check 200 for $29.95, you would type');
  writeln;
  writeln('check, 200, 29.95');
  writeln;
  writeln('and then you would hit the return key.');
  writeln('When you have no more checks to enter, type');
  writeln;
  writeln('no more checks');
  writeln;
  writeln('and then hit the return key.');
  writeln
end;
```

Then, in the main program the user would be given the option of requesting help in entering his or her checks.

```
  writeln('Do you need help in entering your checks?');
  writeln('Type y or n and hit the carriage return.');
  readln(answer);
  writeln;
  if answer <> 'n' then
    helpwithchecks;
```

Obviously, this kind of information can be included in a user manual, but think of how much more pleasant the user will find your code if he or she can get help from the program itself, rather than having to look up the information in a manual. Be aware that the user may not know what to do when he or she is in the middle of entering the data. Your program may have to recognize and act on a special help key, even when reading in numeric data.

When dummy-proofing a program, think of the luggage commercial on television where a large gorilla is given a suitcase with which to do what he pleases. The gorilla provides the ultimate test to see if the suitcase can withstand the brutal treatment luggage receives from bellboys in hotels or loading crews at airports. Although we don't really have to worry about an ape throwing our programs around in his cage, we should be prepared for the worst kind of user errors so that our programs will not "fall apart" when they are being run by the user (for more on this, see Proverbs 34 and 43). When a program collapses because it was not dummy-proofed and, thus, did not expect the user's input, who is really the dummy? Think about it!

43 Garbage in, be ready for it.

Computer magazines have run many data-processing "horror stories" about a keypunch error costing a city hundreds of thousands of dollars in tax revenues, a misinterpreted column of a punched card causing a school scheduling system to schedule all the classes in one room, or a programming error causing a consumer to receive a utilities bill for several thousand dollars. Each of these events happened because the programmer, who designed the data-processing code, trusted the input and output data.

Suppose that William Wannabuck, president of a wholesale consumer products distributing company, hired you to write a billing system for his firm, Willy's Warehouses, Inc. You will need to take a careful look at the company inventory and the present billing system to see what kinds of products the company distributes and how large the typical bills are. Because you are contracted to work for Mr. Wannabuck only long enough to complete the billing system, it is important that you remember the user and beware of the data.

After a brief tour of one of the warehouses, you learn that the least expensive item that the firm sells is a $5 garbage can, and the most expensive item is a $20,000 circus tent. Because you are suspicious of the (not unlikely) possibility of a data entry clerk mispunching a key and causing an office furniture purchaser to be billed $50 for a trash can, you add error-checking routines that test the input price to match the item (see the example of the price-validating procedure for Wanda's Wardrobes in Proverb 24).

You may choose to add logic to your program that flags suspicious bills. For example, if the largest bill that Willy's Warehouses, Inc., has ever sent to a customer was for $100,000, and bills over $30,000 are very rare, then you might write a message to the user to bring his or her attention to bills that are very large.

In the software industry, quality-control engineers carefully test programs before they are distributed to see whether these programs can handle user errors. The testing engineer answers the questions that the program asks with ridiculous input to see whether the code can handle the input error. Only after running the code through the toughest of tests can the engineer consider the code both user friendly and guarded against input errors.

Here are a few hints to help you in designing and testing the input portion of your program.

1. Test input data for validity and plausibility. As in the example for Willy's Warehouses, make sure that the input information makes sense. The warehouse billing program should reject an attempt at billing a customer for an item that the company doesn't even sell or an attempt at charging him a higher price for an item than any item in the inventory.

2. Make sure that the input doesn't violate the limits of your program. If, in the billing program for Willy's Warehouses, the company's inventory is kept in a table implemented as an array, make sure that the program writes an error message if the user tries to input more values than the array can hold. Also guard against input values that result in the program trying to compute a value greater than maxint. Provide tests when there is a possibility of overloading a variable, and provide a means for the user to correct the input error.

3. For interactive input, include prompts for your user that explain what is expected, and make the format of the input easy for the user. The interactive billing program for Willy's Warehouses might give the user the following prompts:

```
Enter the transaction date (month-day-year)
                         (for example, 1-15-85)

Enter the customer name (at most 30 characters)

Enter the 9 digit customer billing number

Enter the number of items sold to this customer
```

4. Echo print, that is, write out the input data. This aids in locating errors and associates an output result with the input data that produced it. Let's continue with the interactive billing program (user answers are underlined).

```
Enter the transaction date (month-day-year)
                         (for example, 1-15-85)
2-28-85<ret>

Enter the customer name
Sammy's Circus Company<ret>

Enter the 9 digit customer billing number
372918470<ret>

Enter the number of items sold to this customer
3<ret>

Enter the 5 digit item number and price
99999 $20000.00<ret>

Enter the 5 digit item number and price
32013 $489.95<ret>

Enter the 5 digit item number and price
67452 $74.49<ret>
```

After the user's answers have been input, we echo-print the data, as follows:

```
Date of transaction:       February 28, 1985
Customer:                  Sammy's Circus Company
Customer billing number:   372918470
Number of items sold:      3

Item Number                      Price
   99999                      $20000.00
   32013                        489.95
   67452                         74.49
                              --------
Amount Due                    $20564.44
```

Notice that each user prompt is meaningful and that the responses are echoed back to ensure that the data were entered accurately.

5. Identify and recover from bad input data, if possible. If the data are input interactively, reject the bad data and prompt the user again. For example, suppose the data entry clerk made the following mistake

```
Enter the transaction date (month-day-year)
                      (for example, 1-15-85)

2-29-85<ret>
```

The program should reject the input data and write a message like

```
February 29, 1985 is not a valid date.  Try again.

Enter the transaction date (month-day-year)
                      (for example, 1-15-85)
```

If your input is not interactive but, rather, comes from a file, you must still look for and recover from bad input data; but you cannot rely on an interactive user to help you out. To avoid fireworks in your program, you must decide to do something safe and sane with the input; often, you will have to skip over the bad data and proceed to the next. You should also generate a message that identifies the errors in the data, what is wrong with the data, and what you have done about the errors. For example,

```
Order No. 13722, Willy's Warehouse,
has delivery date February 29, 1985.

February 29, 1985 is not a valid date.
Date changed to March 1, 1985.
```

Even if validated by a separate validation program, the data in your file may still be meaningless in terms of what you are trying to do because the validation program may not be complete. The validation program may check that certain restrictions on the range of values in the file are satisfied, as in the example above for dates. But it may not be able to determine that an order placed on a certain date is invalid if the account is not opened until a subsequent date.

6. Allow defaults. Print the defaulted values with the corresponding input, so that the user can determine what the program did. A default value is one that a program uses if the user chooses not to provide a value. If, for example, Willy's Warehouses processes bills on the same day that customers make purchases, you may choose today's date as the default value for the billing date. You would then write the program so that the data entry operator simply hits the return key on the date prompt if the billing date is the default.

44 Look to the end before you begin.

Before you begin reading in data at the terminal, you will have to provide some means of letting the computer know that you have come to the end of the data. Here are six different methods for indicating the end of a data set in your programs.

1. The number of pieces of data can be built directly into the program through an explicit constant. For example, if you will always be reading in 10 items, then you may choose to hard-wire the number 10 as the number of input items:

```
writeln('Enter the item numbers of 10 items, ',
        'each on a separate line.');
for i := 1 to 10 do
  begin
    writeln('Enter item number ', i:3);
    readln(item[i])
  end;
```

2. The number can be referred to through a **const** declaration. This is a good idea, particularly if the number is used in more than one place in the program. For example,

```
const
  numberofitems = 10;
      .

      .

writeln('Enter the item numbers of', numberofitems:3,
        ' items, each on a separate line.');
for i := 1 to numberofitems do
  begin
    writeln('Enter item number ', i:3);
    readln(item[i])
  end;
```

3. The count can be read from the input data. If the number of items varies and the user knows that number, you can ask the user to give that number before he or she inputs the data. For example,

```
writeln('How many items are there?  ',
        'Enter a non-negative integer.');
writeln('Then enter the item numbers, ',
        'each on a separate line.');
readln(numberofitems);
for i := 1 to numberofitems do
  begin
    writeln('Enter item number ', i:3);
    readln(item[i])
  end;
```

4. The data can be read until a sentinel is encountered. A sentinel is a value that terminates the process of reading in data. It is usually a value that doesn't make sense as regular input data but that the program recognizes as the end-of-data indicator. A sentinel may be used if the user does not know, or does not want to count, the number of items he or she wants to input. Sometimes, zero is used as a sentinel. Here is an example:

```
writeln('Enter the item numbers, ',
        'each on a separate line.');
writeln('Enter 0 when you are finished.');
i := 0;
repeat
  i := i + 1;
  writeln('Enter item number ', i:3);
  readln(item[i])
until item[i] = 0;
```

5. A flag can be used to terminate reading in data. This is sometimes preferred to the use of a sentinel, because a sentinel is treated as data, whereas a flag is not. However, it can be very tedious to input the value of a flag along with each item of data.

```
writeln('Enter the item numbers, ',
        'each on a separate line.');
flag := 'y';
i := 0;
repeat
  i := i + 1;
  writeln('Enter item number ', i:3);
  readln(item[i]);
  writeln('Do you wish to continue?');
  writeln('Type y for yes and n for no.');
  readln(flag)
until flag = 'n';
```

6. The data can be read until the end of file is encountered. If neither you nor the user knows (or wants to count) the number of data items, then the best technique is to use the **while not** eof construct.

```
i := 0;
writeln('Enter item number 1 or end-of-file.');
while not eof and (i < maxi) do
   begin
      i := i + 1;
      readln(item[i]);
      if i < maxi then
         writeln('Enter item number ', i+1:3,
                  'or end-of-file.');
   end;
```

This technique is best because it requires no special action by the user and allows an arbitrary number of data items to be read. Note, however, that on most systems eof can be used with the standard input file only once in a given program. If you have several distinct sets of data to read, you will have to use one of the other methods described instead. Furthermore, if you have trailing blanks at the end of the input file, the fragment above will blow up. See Proverb 54 for a discussion of this point and a user-defined function, endoffile, to use in place of eof when reading integers or real numbers from a textfile[1] and there are trailing blanks.

45 Let your output speak for itself.

Output, when displayed at a terminal or produced on hard copy, should be self-explanatory. The results produced by your program should be presented in a format that is clear, easily understood, and legible. Look at the following mess:

```
                        345659876
1.457040000000000e+03     2    264.350      33.45
                      1.159240000000000e+03
```

---

[1] The one-word usage is a convention established by the IEEE in the *American National Standard Pascal Computer Programming Language* (John Wiley & Sons, New York, 1983).

This might mean something to the original programmer, but it is obviously meaningless to anyone else without explanation of the meaning of each value. The original programmer will also find the output difficult to interpret if he puts it away and reads it again in a couple of months. A better way to present the output is as follows:

```
Social Security Number: 345-65-9876

Number of Dependents: 2

       Gross Pay: $1457.04
     Federal Tax: <$264.35>
       State Tax:  <$33.45>
                   ---------
   Take Home Pay: $1159.24
```

Problems and Projects

1. Consult the manuals for your system regarding the read, readln, write, and writeln procedures. Experiment with the use of these procedures by writing several small programs until you understand how these procedures work on your system.

2. Given the declarations

    ```
    var
        k, l, m, n: integer;
    ```

    and the input data

    ```
    7   25<eoln>
    39   12<eoln>
    <eof>
    ```

    what is the value of each variable after execution of each of the following input sequences? Do any of these input sequences lead to an error caused by attempting a read or readln when eof is true?

(a)   read (k , l) ;
        read (m , n) ;

(b)   readln (k , l , m , n) ;

(c)   readln (k) ;
        readln (l) ;
        readln (m) ;
        readln (n) ;

(d)   readln (k , l) ;
        readln (m , n) ;

3.   Write input commands to read in the following data, using meaningful identifiers that you declare. A card is the same as one line of input. Each piece of information is separated from the next by one blank space.

(a) A payroll identification card containing a social security number, followed by a department number (integer). After the payroll identification card, there is a time card containing a deduction code (character), followed by the number of hours worked on each day of the week (five integers).

(b) A grade card containing a student identification number (integer), a classification (character), and four grades (four characters).

4.   Suppose you are given the declarations

          var
             ch1, ch2, ch3: char;

and the input string

           hi!<eoln>

If each of the following input sequences occurs in a program before any other read or write operations are done, what is the value of each variable after the sequence has been executed? Try each of these sequences on your system to check your answers.

(a) `readln;`
   `read(ch1,ch2,ch3);`

(b) `readln(ch1,ch2,ch3);`

(c) `readln(ch1);`
   `readln(ch2);`
   `readln(ch3);`

5. Proverb 44 describes six different methods of indicating the end of the input data. For each of these six methods, outline an application for which you feel it would be the most appropriate method and an application for which it would be quite unsuitable.

6. Write a procedure that interrogates users for Willie Liker's Fly-by-Night Computer Dating Service (see Proverb 17). The user will be asked his or her name, followed by 10 yes or no questions, the answers to which will be stored in a one-dimensional array. The procedure that you write must accept input from relatively inexperienced users, must never abort on bad input, must allow users to confirm or modify their input, and must provide very explanatory output messages.

7. Write a Pascal program that enables two players to play tic tac toe interactively. First, it will display the rules of the game and a blank tic tac toe board, with an explanation of how the players will designate their moves. Your program will then request moves from the two players, display the updated board after each move, and notify the players when someone has won or if there is a draw. At the end of the game it will ask the players whether they want to play again. Make your program user friendly! Have it check for input errors and allow players to re-enter their moves.

6
Auxiliary
Data Storage

Files are collections of data that are stored not in the main memory of the computer but, rather, on auxiliary storage media, most often on magnetic disks. Data stored as arrays or records in the main memory of the computer are kept only during the execution of the program that uses them. Data stored in files on an auxiliary storage device can be kept for days, weeks, or even years!

Files are really nothing new—you have been editing, saving, and deleting files ever since you first logged into a computer. They provide the means of communication between your program and the outside environment. They enable you to supply input to a program and to store a program's output and, indeed, to store the program itself. Now you're going to learn how to access and manipulate files within a Pascal program.

150

In this chapter we will discuss some proverbs that will help you in creating files and also in subsequently accessing data from the files that you have created. We will consider nontext files and also textfiles, which are substructured into lines by end-of-line markers and are therefore handled differently from nontext files. The proverbs in this chapter are designed to help you find the use of files in Pascal programming a more pleasurable experience.

46 Files are for keeps.

To save and to keep track of important records and documents, businesses have filing cabinets in which they store their files of information. When programmers need to save important information, they store this information in files on magnetic disks or tapes. Then, instead of having to enter the data for a program each time the program is run, they can simply access the information from their files.

Many businesses these days also store much of their information in files on disks or tapes instead of in filing cabinets. Consider the case of Here's Where They Are (HWTA), Inc., a company that compiles lists of addresses of people who purchase particular products, watch particular TV shows, live in particular neighborhoods, etc. HWTA sells these lists to catalog companies, time-share companies, and other marketing organizations. Their data entry technicians enter the data, which have been gathered by the company, into a computer where the data are stored in files. Here is a representation of a few components of the file that contains the addresses of people who recently purchased German sports cars.

Skip Speedster	2 Skidmark Drive	Overdrive, OR 87654	Porsche 911
Heavy Foot	The Road	Roadster, RI 01234	Mercedes 450SL
Rick Racer	1 Fast Lane	Highgear, HI 99999	Porsche 944

When HWTA has a request from a customer in the auto customizing business who wants a list of the addresses in this file, the company sends the customer a listing of the information in the file. They may even send the customer a copy of the file on a disk or tape, if their two computers read and write files using the same formats. The customer, then, does not have to reenter the information into his own computer in order to process it.

The files that HWTA keeps are "permanent" to the extent that they exist after execution of the program that created them. As information is gathered, HWTA can update their files, but they must be careful to maintain consistency in these files. This can be a difficult problem! As you become skilled in programming, your programs will become less oriented toward calculation and more oriented toward the storage and retrieval of information in files. You may wish to take a course in file management and, perhaps, also a course in database management.

47 Files are the parameters to your program.

Files are frequently used to store data produced by one program for subsequent input to another program. For example, the programmer for Here's Where They Are, Inc., could write a program that takes as input the file of people who recently purchased German sports cars and produces as output a file of people who recently purchased some particular German sports car, such as the Porsche.

In Pascal, files that exist before the start of a program and/or after its end must be passed as parameters in the program heading and must be declared in the outermost declaration block of the program, as in the following example:

```pascal
program example(infile, outfile);
type
   filetype = file of real;
var
   infile, outfile: filetype;
begin
```

Files can also be used strictly as data structures internal to a program when a program needs more memory space for temporary data storage than is available in the computer's main memory. Such files are not listed in the program heading and disappear when the program terminates.

In Pascal, a file consists of a sequence of components, much like an array. However, a file may be arbitrarily long (its size is constrained only by the available disk or tape storage space); an array, on the other hand, is fixed in length and relatively small (its size is constrained by the available space in memory). Furthermore, the components of a file must be processed in a fixed order, whereas the components of an array may be accessed directly by subscript.

Information in a file in Pascal must be stored and accessed sequentially, just like songs on a cassette tape. When you record an album on a tape, you record the songs sequentially, appending them one after the other. A file in Pascal is created in a similar way, by writing or appending new components to the end of the file. When the file is subsequently read, the components are read one after the other from the beginning of the file, in the order in which they were written.

Just as only one song on a tape is accessible to the listener at any one time, only one component of a file is accessible to a program. We can imagine a marker, associated with the file, that points to the currently accessible component, a copy of which is contained in a buffer, or intermediate storage place, in memory. We can access data in the buffer and also store data in the buffer, so that it can be appended to the file. The file buffer is sometimes also referred to as a file window because, through it, we can access and store data in the file. We will talk more about this buffer variable and how to use it in the next proverb.

48 Files contain data, and data are structured; think of your files as data structures.

Pascal provides a standard file type text. Textfiles are composed of characters that are separated into lines by special end-of-line characters. We can also create nontext or binary files, the components of which may be, for example, integers, arrays, or records.

All files, except for the standard input and output files, must be declared as variables. When a file f is declared, a file buffer variable, denoted by f↑, is automatically created. It contains the file component currently pointed to by the file marker (see Fig. 6.1) and may be used in a program like any other variable.

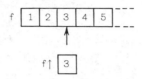

Figure 6.1 File marker and file buffer variable.

As an example of the declaration of a textfile, consider the following:

```
var
    formletter: text;
```

Notice that there is no need to declare the type text first. When a nontext file is declared, on the other hand, the type of the file must be specified. For example,

```
type
    astring = array[1..30] of char;
    clientrecord = record
                        name, address, telephone: astring;
                   end;
    clientfile = file of clientrecord;
var
    client: clientrecord;
    clients: clientfile;
```

Here, clients is a file of clients' records, and clients↑ is the record currently pointed to by the file marker. The fields of this record are accessed in the usual way with a field selector. For example, clients↑.name is a string a particular client's name and clients↑.telephone is his or her telephone number. Furthermore, clients↑.name[1] is the first character of the client's name, etc.

As another example, consider

```
type
    probabilitymatrix = array[1..8,1..8] of real;
    probabilityfile = file of probabilitymatrix;
var
    chances: probabilityfile;
```

Notice, here, that chances is a file of probability matrices, that chances↑ is the matrix pointed to by the file marker, and also that chances↑[2,3] is the entry in the second row and third column of the matrix chances↑.

When integer, real, or boolean values are stored in or accessed from a textfile, these values must be converted between their internal numerical and their external character representations. This conversion can be avoided by keeping these values in their internal representation, in nontext or binary files. Nontext files of types integer, real, and boolean are used for speed, size, and accuracy because their values need not be encoded or decoded individually, because they can be stored in a compact manner, and because, in the case of real numbers, they are more accurate.

Although textfiles can be created with an editor or printed directly, nontext files cannot be created, read, or printed except by a Pascal program. Components of nontext files are stored in binary form according to the particular internal representation of your computer. A listing of a nontext file in its internal binary representation will be meaningless to you. You will need to design a little program to create a nontext file and to print such a file for each kind that you declare. We will show you how to do this in Proverb 50.

49 Files have a beginning and an end; let's start at the very beginning.

Before you use a file it must be "opened," that is, the file must be initialized so that the file marker is positioned at the beginning of the file. The standard input and output files are automatically opened for you. Any other files must be opened for reading by reset, or opened for writing by rewrite. In standard Pascal, files are "closed" automatically for you (which includes writing a character or characters to indicate the end of the file), but on some systems (often on microcomputer systems) you will have to close each file that you create explicitly by a statement in your program.

To create a file f, the file must first be prepared for writing by executing

rewrite(f)

The procedure call rewrite(f) initializes f to an empty file containing no components. (**Warning**: Any existing information in f is destroyed!) The next value written to f then becomes the first component of f, and subsequent values are written to the end of f.

Once we have created a file, we can read from it. Before starting to read, we must prepare the file for reading by executing

reset(f)

The procedure call reset(f) moves the file marker to the beginning of the file and, if f is not empty, transfers the contents of the first component of the file into the buffer variable f↑ (see Fig. 6.2). If f is empty, f↑ is undefined.

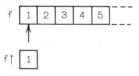

Figure 6.2 After reset is called.

To illustrate the use of rewrite and reset, let's consider the problem of concatenating two files, that is, appending one to the end of the other. To do this we must introduce a third file. We copy the components of the first file to the third file, reading from the first and writing to the third. Then, we copy the components of the second file to the third file, reading from the second and writing to the third. Note that we must reset the files from which we are reading and rewrite the file to which we are writing.

```
(* This procedure returns file3 which is the result *)
(* of appending file2 to the end of file1.          *)
procedure concatenate(var file1, file2, file3: filetype);
begin
   reset(file1);
   reset(file2);
   rewrite(file3);

   while not eof(file1) do
     begin
       file3↑ := file1↑;
       get(file1);
       put(file3)
     end;

   while not eof(file2) do
     begin
       file3↑ := file2↑;
       get(file2);
       put(file3)
     end
 end;
```

Don't confuse reset and rewrite. Remember, reset puts us at the beginning of a file ready for reading and rewrite gives us an empty file ready for writing. If you try to read a file that has not been reset or try to write without first calling rewrite, your program will crash.[1]

You must also be very careful not to misplace reset or rewrite in your program code. If, when you print out the contents of your file, you keep getting the same piece of data or you only get the last piece of data you entered, chances are you included rewrite or reset in a loop that was intended to read or write your file. The rewrite and reset procedures should be called before entering the loop.

---

[1]Crash—terminate with an error message from the operating system.

50 Get and put are simple, if you learn to use them.

The basic commands for accessing files are get and put. Although these procedures take a file as a parameter, it is the file buffer variable that provides access to the data.

The first stage in the use of a file is its creation. To create a file f, we must first prepare it for writing, using the standard procedure call rewrite(f). Then we write the successive components to the file, using the put operation. More precisely, to write a component to a file f, we first assemble the data into the buffer variable f↑ and then call the procedure put, that is,

$$f↑ := newdata;$$
$$put(f);$$

The procedure call put(f) appends the value of the buffer variable f↑ to the end of the file f and advances the file marker. The value of f↑ becomes undefined, ready for the next data to be assigned to it.

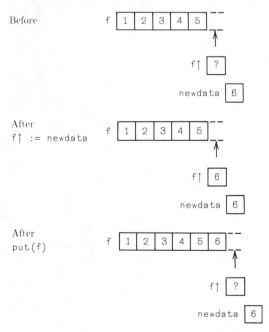

Figure 6.3 Appending a new component to the end of a file.

Let's consider a case study. Mermaids in the Drink, Inc., (an exotic company, even by Californian standards) paints murals on the sides and bottoms of swimming pools. They maintain a file of records with the names, addresses, and telephone numbers of their clients. They use the following program to create the file.

```
(* This program creates a file of client records  *)
(* with their names, addresses and phone numbers. *)
program createafile(input, output, clients);
type
   astring =  array[1..30] of char;
   clientrecord = record
                    name, address, telephone: astring
                  end;
   clientfile = file of clientrecord;
var
   clients: clientfile;
   answer: char;

   procedure createarecord(var r: clientrecord);
   var
      i: 0..30;
   begin (* Createarecord *)
      (* Initialize the name and address to blanks. *)
      for i := 1 to 30 do
        begin
           r.name[i]  := ' ';
           r.address[i] := ' ';
           r.telephone[i] := ' '
        end;
      writeln('Enter the name of the client.');
      i := 0;
      while not eoln and (i < 30) do
        begin
           i := i + 1;
           read(r.name[i])
        end;
      readln;
```

```
    writeln('Enter the address of the client.');
    i := 0;
    while not eoln and (i < 30) do
       begin
          i := i + 1;
          read(r.address[i])
       end;
    readln;
    writeln('Enter the phone number of the client.');
    i := 0;
    while not eoln and (i < 13) do
       begin
          i := i + 1;
          read(r.telephone[i])
       end;
    readln
  end; (* Createarecord *)

begin (* Createafile *)
  rewrite(clients);
  answer := 'y';
  while answer <> 'n' do
     begin
        writeln('Do you want to enter another client?');
        writeln('Enter y or n and then return.');
        readln(answer);
        if answer <> 'n' then
           begin
              createarecord(clients↑);
              put(clients)
           end
     end
end. (* Createafile *)
```

Notice that each of the fields of the record—clients↑.name, clients↑.address, clients↑.telephone—must be prepared first, and then the entire record is put into the file all at once.

Once we have created a file, we can read the data back from it. After resetting a file, we can read the data in its first component, which is available in the buffer variable f↑. Then we can move on to the second component by calling the procedure get. For example,

```
currentdata := f↑;
get(f);
```

The procedure call get(f) advances the file marker to the next component of the file and updates the buffer variable to provide access to that component (see Fig. 6.4).

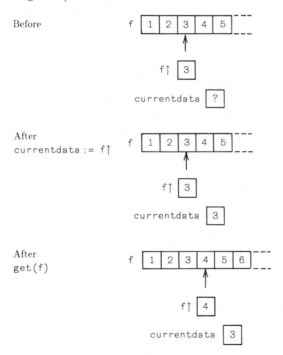

Figure 6.4 Accessing a component of a file.

If the file marker is pointing to the last component of the file f and get(f) is executed, eof(f) becomes true and the buffer variable f↑ becomes undefined. A further call get(f), when eof(f) is true and f↑ is undefined, causes a run-time error.

Now let's look at the program that Mermaids in the Drink, Inc., uses to print the file of records of their clients. As with the program used to create a file, all of the detail is in printing the components. The actual get and put operations are very simple. In this case, all we need to do is to print the name, address, and phone number from each record. Note the typical structure of the loop. Initially, we must reset the client file, placing the first record in the file buffer. Then, we have a while loop testing for eof, within which we process the record and then use get to advance to the next record.

```
(* This program prints the names, addresses,   *)
(* and phone numbers contained in the records *)
(* of the file clients.                         *)

program printafile(output, clients);
type
   astring = array[1..30] of char;
   clientrecord = record
                    name, address, telephone: astring
                  end;
   clientfile = file of clientrecord;
var
   clients: clientfile;
```

```pascal
procedure printarecord(r: clientrecord);
var
  i: 1..30;
begin (* Printarecord *)
  (* Print the client's name. *)
  for i := 1 to 30 do
    write(r.name[i]);
  writeln;

  (* Print the client's address. *)
  for i := 1 to 30 do
    write(r.address[i]);
  writeln;

  (* Print the client's phone number. *)
  for i := 1 to 13 do
    writeln(r.telephone[i]);
  writeln;
  writeln
end; (* Printarecord *)
begin (* Printafile *)
  writeln('The names, addresses, and phone numbers ',
          'of the clients are:');
  writeln;
  reset(clients);
  while not eof(clients) do
    begin
      printarecord(clients↑);
      get(clients)
    end
end. (* Printafile *)
```

Note that according to the standard, Pascal allows you to use read and write with nontext files (as well as with textfiles). However, because these do not work on some systems, we prefer to use the more basic get and put operations with nontext files.

51 End with neither a bang nor a whimper.

The boolean function eof is used to determine whether or not the end of a file has been reached. In particular, eof(f) is true when the file marker is advanced past the last component of the file and, also, when the file is empty.

When eof(f) is true, f↑ is undefined, and if you try to access f↑, your program will crash and you will get a run-time error message like

> Tried to read past eof

Thus, it is important that you check that eof(f) is false before using f↑. For example, the following **repeat** loop, which is intended to copy a file, will result in a run-time error if the original file is empty.

```
(* This fragment copies a file, *)
(* one component at a time.      *)
reset(original);
rewrite(copy);
repeat
  copy↑ := original↑;
  get(original);
  put(copy)
until eof(original);
```

In place of the **repeat** loop, a **while** loop should be used to ensure that eof(original) is false before accessing original↑.

```
(* This fragment copies a file, *)
(* one component at a time.      *)
reset(original);
rewrite(copy);
while not eof(original) do
  begin
    copy↑ := original↑;
    get(original);
    put(copy)
  end;
```

When reading from two files simultaneously, you must check that you are not at the end of either while continuing to read. If you check only one and the other is shorter, you will again have a run-time error. Even if the files are meant to be the same length, you should still check both. It is much better to be able to issue your own error message, such as "bad data—bag the results" than to have your program bomb.[2]

In the following procedure, which might be used, for example, in an airline reservation system or in the banking industry, one file (the master file) is updated by merging information from a second file (the transaction file). A specific field, the key, is used for ordering the records in the two files. The two files are merged while preserving the order of the keys.

```
(* This procedure updates a master file by merging    *)
(* records from a transaction file in such a way that  *)
(* the ordering of the records by keys is preserved    *)
(* in the updated file.                                *)
procedure merge(var master,transaction,updated:filetype);
begin
  reset(master);
  reset(transaction);
  rewrite(updated);
  while not eof(master) and not eof(transaction) do
    begin
      if master↑.key < transaction↑.key then
        begin
          updated↑ := master↑;
          get(master)
        end
      else
        begin
          updated↑ := transaction↑;
          get(transaction)
        end;
      put(updated)
    end;
```

---

[2]Bomb—terminate with an error message from the operating system.

```
(* At this point we're at the end of one  *)
(* of the two files, and we need to copy   *)
(* the remaining components of the other,  *)
(* if any.                                  *)

while not eof(master) do
  begin
    updated↑ := master↑;
    get(master);
    put(updated)
  end;
while not eof(transaction) do
  begin
    updated↑ := transaction↑;
    get(transaction);
    put(updated)
  end
end;
```

Remember, eof(f) is true after reset if the file f is empty, and when read or get has moved the file marker past the last component of the file. To prevent a run-time error when accessing a file, check that eof(f) is false before executing read or get.

52 To change is to copy.

To copy a file, we can't simply assign one file variable to another, because a file is external to memory and only the file buffer variable is accessible in memory. Just as we copy one song after another when making a copy of an album on cassette tape, we must read a component from one file and write it to a second file, copying one component at a time.

Furthermore, we can't alternate between reading and writing individual components to the same file. To insert a new component into a file, to modify an existing component of a file, or to delete a component from a file, we must create a second file and copy components from the first file into the second.

Suppose, for example, that we wish to maintain a file of restaurants and their ratings. Such a file, called the "Yum Yum List," is maintained by the students at Stanford University.

If we wish to insert a new component containing information about a new restaurant that has just opened, we must go to the beginning of the file, read from it, and write to another file until we get to the point where we want to make the insertion. We then write the new component to the second file. Then, we continue reading from the first, writing to the second, etc.

```
(* This procedure inserts a new component    *)
(* into a file by copying the components of *)
(* the file and inserting the new component *)
(* after the designated component.          *)
(*                                          *)
(* It calls the function placetoinsert and  *)
(* the procedure createarecord.             *)
procedure insertafter(keyname: astring;
          var current, revised: restaurantfile);
begin
  reset(current);
  rewrite(revised);
  while not eof(current) do
    begin
      revised↑ := current↑;
      put(revised);
      if placetoinsert(keyname, current↑) then
        begin
          createarecord(revised↑);
          put(revised)
        end;
      get(current)
    end
end;
```

If the rating of one of the restaurants drops from, say, four stars to three stars, we must modify the required component and insert it into the file, copying the entire file in the process. More specifically, we first make a copy of the component. If no alteration is required, we simply put the record unchanged into the second file. If we wish to modify certain fields, we change the fields of the record and then put the modified record into the second file.

```
(* This procedure modifies a file by copying   *)
(* its components, and modifying and replacing *)
(* the designated components.                  *)
(*                                             *)
(* It calls the function componentisok and     *)
(* the procedure modifycomponent.              *)
procedure modifyfile(var current,
                     revised: restaurantfile);
begin
  reset(current);
  rewrite(revised);
  while not eof(current) do
    begin
      revised↑ := current↑;
      if not componentisok(revised↑) then
        modifycomponent(revised↑);
      put(revised);
      get(current)
    end
end;
```

If, say, the Department of Public Health closes one of the restaurants (perhaps because the "Bears" got into it), it should be deleted from the file. Again, we must go to the beginning of the file, read from it, and write to a second file until we get to the appropriate component. We skip over the component that we wish to delete and then continue reading a component, writing a component, etc., as in the following procedure:

```
(* This procedure deletes components from a file    *)
(* by copying the file, one component at a time,     *)
(* except for the components to be deleted.          *)
(*                                                   *)
(* The procedure calls the function placetodelete.   *)

procedure delete(var current,revised:restaurantfile);
begin
    reset(current);
    rewrite(revised);
    while not eof(current) do
        begin
            if not placetodelete(current↑) then
                begin
                    revised↑ := current↑;
                    put(revised)
                end;
            get(current)
        end
end;
```

The examples above also illustrate that files may be passed as parameters to procedures and functions. However, they must be passed as reference (or **var**) parameters, because they are external to memory and only one component at a time is accessible and, also, because they may be extremely large. If a file is passed as a value parameter, a copy of the entire file has to be made on entry to the procedure or function. Although a file f cannot be passed as a value parameter, the file buffer variable f↑ can be passed as a value parameter because, in this case, just a single component of the file is copied.

53 Hear the word on text.

A textfile is a file of char, substructured into lines by so-called end-of-line markers. Textfiles and nontext files differ in that nothing separates the components of a nontext file, whereas the components of a textfile are divided up into lines by these special end-of-line markers. Although the physical representation varies from machine to machine, Figure 6.5 shows what a textfile t looks like to the user:

Figure 6.5 End-of-line and end-of-file markers in a textfile.

The procedures get and put and the function eof, which we considered previously, can be used with textfiles. Indeed, the standard procedures read and write, which are defined for textfiles, do use get and put. For a textfile t and a variable ch of type char, the procedure call

$$\text{write}(t, ch)$$

is equivalent to

```
t↑ := ch;
put(t)
```

For a textfile t and a variable ch of type char, the procedure call

$$\text{read}(t, ch)$$

is equivalent to

```
ch := t↑;
get(t)
```

In addition, the procedures readln and writeln and the function eoln are specifically defined for textfiles to handle end-of-line markers. (These are not defined for nontext files, but then who needs them when nontext files don't contain end-of-line markers.) The end-of-line markers are put into a textfile by writeln, and we can skip past them using readln. The procedure call

$$\text{writeln}(t)$$

appends an end-of-line marker to the textfile t. Similarly,

$$\text{readln}(t)$$

advances the file marker past the characters on the current line, if any, and past the special end-of-line marker to the first character on the next line (or to the end of the file if there is no next line). It is defined in terms of get, as follows:

```
while not eoln(t) do
   get(t);
get(t);
```

If the special end-of-line marker itself is read, it is converted into a blank before it is stored. Thus, if we subsequently print it, a blank space will appear.

To determine when we're at the end of a line, we use the eoln function. For a textfile t, eoln(t) is true if the file buffer variable t↑ contains the special end-of-line marker and is false everywhere else.

Consider, now, the following example in which we copy one textfile to another, character by character, while preserving the line structure of the file that we're copying.

```
(* Copy infile by reading from infile *)
(* and writing to outfile.             *)

reset(infile);
rewrite(outfile);
while not eof(infile) do
   begin
      while not eoln(infile) do
         begin
            read(infile,ch);
            write(outfile,ch)
         end;
      readln(infile);
      writeln(outfile)
   end;
```

Notice the placement of the read inside the inner loop. We test for the end of line before attempting to read the first character. Notice, also, the placement of the readln and writeln after the inner loop. The readln takes us past the next end-of-line marker in the file that we are reading, and the writeln puts an end-of-line marker into the file that we are writing.

Notice, also, that infile is used as a parameter to read, readln, eof, and eoln and that outfile is used as a parameter to write and writeln. If the file name is omitted from any of the procedures or functions that refer to reading in values (namely read, readln, eof, or eoln), the standard input file is used by default. Likewise, if the file name is omitted from either of the write procedures, the default is the standard output file.

A special case of the preceding is to read from the file infile and to write it to the standard output file, that is, to print it at the terminal. Hildegard wrote the following piece of code:

```
(* Read from the file infile and *)
(* print it at the terminal.     *)
reset(infile);
while not eof do
  begin
    while not eoln do
      begin
        read(infile,ch);
        write(ch)
      end;
    readln(infile);
    writeln
  end;
```

However, her fragment resulted in the run-time error message

```
                Tried to read past eof
```

because she forgot to include the name of the file infile as a parameter to the functions eof and eoln. Remember, if you use eof or eoln without a parameter, it is the standard input file that is tested. The fragment should be rewritten, as follows:

```
(* Read from the file infile and *)
(* print it at the terminal.       *)
reset(infile);
while not eof(infile) do
  begin
    while not eoln(infile) do
      begin
        read(infile,ch);
        write(ch)
      end;
    readln(infile);
    writeln
  end;
```

When you are reading from and writing to textfiles, make sure that you can explain every blank space and every empty line that appears, as well as every full line that should appear but doesn't. Make sure your textfile routines can handle these special cases.

- Blanks at the beginning of a line.
- Blanks at the end of a line.
- Lines that are empty.

54 Reading 1 2 3 is as easy as A B C.

In the previous proverb we considered textfiles as files of characters, which are read from and written to the file one at a time. Although files usually allow only one component at a time to be read or written and this component must be of the type declared for the file, textfiles are usually handled somewhat differently. You can, for example, write an integer or real number to the standard output file and also read from the standard input file into an integer or real variable that you have declared.

When you write an integer or real number to a textfile, the write statement automatically converts the number into a string of characters. Similarly, when you read from a textfile into an integer or real variable, the read statement automatically converts a string of characters into the corresponding numerical value.

The statement `write(t,ch)` writes a single character `ch` to the textfile `t`. But when `write(t,v)` is used with a variable `v` of type `real`, `integer`, `boolean`, or `string`,[3] the value must first be converted to a sequence of characters, and then these characters are written to the file.

Likewise, the statement `read(t,ch)` reads one character, the character currently pointed to by the file marker. However, when `read(t,v)` is used with a variable `v` of type `integer` or `real`, the read procedure must read an entire number, which may be represented by many characters. In this case, the file marker is advanced past blank and end-of-line markers to the first character (+, -, or digit) of the number. The rest of the characters that make up the number are then read, and the character sequence representing the number is converted into a numerical value.

Suppose that we're reading integer values `v` from a textfile and there are trailing blanks (or end-of-line markers) at the end of the file. Although the following fragment of code looks good, it will not work if there are trailing blanks.

```
while not eof(t) do
  begin
    read(t,v);
    process(v)
  end;
```

When the last number has been read, we are not yet at the end of the file; thus, the read procedure is invoked and it reads past the trailing blanks all the way to the end of the file, looking for the start of a number. When the read procedure tries to read the end-of-file marker, the program crashes with an error message like

```
                Bad data found on integer read
```

To solve this problem, we might consider the following fragment, which is intended to skip over blanks.

```
while not eof(t) and (t↑ = ' ') do
    get(t);
if not eof(t) then
    read(t,v);
```

---

[3]String—a packed array of characters.

This loop may result in a run-time error, because at the end of the file, when eof (t) is true, t↑ will still be accessed if the boolean expression is fully evaluated. We can eliminate this problem easily if we write the loop slightly differently.

```
while not eof(t) do
   if t↑ = ' ' then
      get(t);
if not eof(t) then
   read(t,v);
```

However, this code fragment suffers from a different problem. If t↑ does not contain a blank and we're not at the end of the file, we have an infinite loop! Now let's consider a correct solution to this problem.

```
(* This function reads past blanks and end of line  *)
(* markers and determines when the end of the file  *)
(* has been reached. It should be used when reading *)
(* a textfile that contains integers or reals.      *)
function endoffile(var t: text): boolean;
var
   done: boolean;
begin
   done := false;
   while not done do
      if eof(t) then
         begin
            endoffile := true;
            done := true
         end
      else if t↑ = ' ' then
         get(t)
      else
         begin
            endoffile := false;
            done := true
         end
end;
```

When you are reading integer or real values from a textfile t, you should use endoffile(t) in place of eof(t) to eliminate the risk that you might read from the file even though there are no more values in it.

Problems and Projects

1. Given the file f illustrated below, what is printed when each of the following fragments is executed? If you need to review reset and get, see Proverbs 49 and 50.

   (a)   reset(f);   (b)   reset(f);
          get(f);   writeln(f↑.data);
          writeln(f↑.data);   get(f);
          get(f);   writeln(f↑.data);
          writeln(f↑.data);

f	1	2	3	4	5	\<eof\>

2. Computer users often find that they have two (or more) versions of the same file and that they need to know whether the two versions are identical. For example, a user who has just copied a file needs to be assured that the copying has been done successfully. Write a program that compares two textfiles to determine whether they are identical. Review the discussion of textfiles in Proverb 53, if necessary.

3. Explain what happens if the following code fragment is executed when (a) the file f is empty or (b) the file marker is pointing to the last component of the file.

                 writeln(f↑.data);
                 get(f);
                 writeln(f↑.data);

4. In assembling its new phone directory, the Chatterbox Phone Company has records for its customers, which contain the following information: last name, first name, middle initial, address, and telephone number. Write a program that reads in these records from the keyboard, stores them in an array, writes them out to the screen, and then writes them to a file. The file should be a file of records, not a textfile. Think of your file as a data structure!

   Now write a program that reads the file of records created by the first program, places the records into an array, sorts them in the array in alphabetic order (last name, first name, middle initial), writes the sorted records to the screen, and then writes them to the file in alphabetic order.

5. The following program fragment is intended to write out all nonblank characters in a textfile t. Explain why it fails to do so. Rewrite the fragment so that it is correct.

   ```
   reset(t);
   read(t,ch);
   while not eof(t) do
     begin
       if ch <> ' ' then
         write(ch);
       read(t,ch)
     end;
   ```

6. Write a program to implement an electronic bulletin board for the students at your university. Such a bulletin board could be used to leave messages regarding rides wanted, cars for sale, apartments for rent, part-time jobs available, etc. The bulletin board will be implemented as a file with certain operations defined on it; specifically, your program will allow students to

   (a) Post notices on the bulletin board (enter them into the file).

   (b) Obtain a summary listing of all the notices in the file.

   (c) Access and print selected notices from the file.

The summary should give the name of the individual who posted the notice, the date of posting, and a brief description (50 characters or less) of the contents of the notice.

7. The following program fragment is intended to read a textfile t, each line of which contains an integer, and to find the sum of all the integers in the file. Explain why it is incorrect. Write a program fragment that correctly finds the sum. See Proverb 54 for help.

```
reset(t);
sum := 0;
while not eof(t) do
   begin
      read(t, num);
      sum := sum + num
   end;
```

8. The Bohemian Browser, a national chain of bookstores, needs a management information system to keep track of their books. The system is to use a file of records, each of which contains the following information about a book: title, author(s), publisher (name, date, location), ISBN (a string of the form *d-ddd-ddddd-d*, where *d* is a digit), and list price. To develop this system for the Browser, first write a small program to create such a file of records. The file should contain records for at least 20 books. Then, write a second program that acts as an information retrieval system and allows the user to

   (a) Print all information about a book with (i) a given title or (ii) a given ISBN.

   (b) Print a list of books (i) written by a given author or (ii) published by a given publisher in a given year.

   If you need help, read Proverbs 47 to 50 again.

9. As discussed in Proverb 54, the standard read procedure automatically converts a character string into a real (integer) when it is reading into a variable of type real (integer). Likewise, the standard write procedure automatically converts a real (integer) value stored

in a variable of type real (integer) into a character string before it is output. Assuming that these features do not exist, write your own read and write procedures to perform these conversions for real numbers. Your procedures should be capable of handling real numbers in both decimal and exponential format. Thus, you should provide two procedures:

procedure realread(s: astring; **var** x: real);

procedure realwrite(x: real; fieldwidth,
        decimalplaces: nonnegint; **var** s: astring);

Your read procedure should take some appropriate action if an error occurs in the input string. Your write procedure should convert the real number to exponential format if the field width and number of decimal places are both zero.

10. Write a Pascal program using procedures and self-defined external files to produce a personalized letter. First, create a file that contains the letter as it is given below with the $ signs followed by digits.

```
$1 $2 $3
$4 $5
$6 $7 $8

Dear $1:

For a limited time we are offering you a $10
credit card.   You and all the $3 family will be able
to use this credit card at any $10 in
$6.   Many of your neighbors on $5 have already
obtained their cards.   To receive your credit card
from the $10, simply fill out, sign, and return
the enclosed application form.

Respectfully,

$11
Consumer Service Manager
```

Next, create a file that contains the names and addresses of prospective credit card customers. The date and the names of the department store and consumer service manager will be input at the terminal. Your program will replace the $ signs followed by digits in the letter above with corresponding data, such as

```
$1      $2 $3                    $9
Maria E. Lopez               May 15, 1986
$4    $5                       $10
1492 A Street                 Big Department Store
$6              $7 $8          $11
Los Angeles, CA 91234         Richard Hughes
```

and will print a personalized letter for each of the persons whose names and addresses occur in the file that you created.

11. The Bank of Big Bucks keeps a file of records for the checking accounts of its customers, all oil men. Each record contains the following information: (a) the customer's name, (b) account number, (c) starting balance, (d) number of deposits, (e) an array of records for deposits (each record consists of the amount of deposit and its date), (f) number of withdrawals, (g) an array of records for withdrawals (each record consists of a check number, the amount of the check, and the date of withdrawal), and (h) ending balance. Write a small program to create such a file of records, with the starting balance and the numbers of deposits and withdrawals set to zero for each customer. Assume that the bank has at least three customers.

Now write a (much larger) program to update the checking accounts for the customers of the bank and to produce an end-of-month statement for each customer. The program will accept as input at a terminal the deposits and withdrawals during the month, together with the dates of those transactions and the number of each check. It will find the total deposits and withdrawals during the month and the final balance for each customer. The program will update the file with all of this information and will produce as output an end-of-month statement containing the updated information. The checks are to be printed in increasing order of check number. If a check has not cleared the bank by the end of the month, a field of asterisks is to be printed. The program will also produce a file for the next month, with the starting balance of the next month initialized to the ending balance of the current month and with the numbers of deposits and withdrawals set to zero. You will encounter this program again in Chapter 9, Problem 8, and also in Chapter 11, Problem 3.

12. As the president of your local computing club, the Bug Byters, you need to determine a meeting time for the club. You'll want to pick a time so that all the members can be present. For each member of the club, you have a two-dimensional array that indicates whether the member is free at a certain hour on a certain day of the week or whether he or she is in class or at work. Write a Pascal program to find a meeting time for the club. Use a file of arrays. Assume that there are, at most, 20 members in the club.

13. Write an automated grading program for your instructor that prepares and maintains a file of records for the students in your class. Each record in the file is to contain a student's name, ID number, scores on the exams and assignments given during the term, and final weighted average. The program should provide a menu of options that allow your instructor to

(a) Add new students.

(b) Drop students.

(c) Record new scores (missed tests or assignments score a zero).

(d) Change incorrect scores.

(e) Compute each student's final grade as a weighted average of his or her scores on the exams and assignments.

(f) Print the name of each student along with his or her ID number, scores on the exams and assignments, and final weighted average.

Remember that to change a file, you must copy it (see Proverb 52). In Chapter 11, Problem 5, you will be asked to write user documentation for this program, so start thinking about it now!

7
Recursion

Recursion is a method of definition in which a concept is defined, either directly or indirectly, in terms of itself. If you have ever been to a fun house at a carnival and looked at mirrors set facing one another, each reflecting the other to infinite depth, then you have caught a glimpse of recursion.

In Pascal, recursion is used to define procedures and functions by making the effects of the procedure, or the result of the function, depend (either directly or indirectly) on a further call of that same procedure or function. Thus, one call depends on another call, which depends on another call, etc., but (unlike the mirrors at the fun house, which reflect each other indefinitely) these calls must eventually terminate.

Recursion is one of the most powerful techniques in modern programming languages for simplifying the design of programs. Skillful and appropriate use of recursion is one of the signs of real mastery of the art of programming in Pascal!

55 Solve your problems gracefully and gradually; think recursively.

Recursion enables us to develop clear, concise, elegant solutions to certain kinds of programming problems. It increases the complexity of the problems that we can handle without becoming confused by detail and enables us to develop programs that might otherwise be quite cumbersome and obscure.

Recursive solutions are particularly appropriate when the solution to a problem can be expressed in terms of a simpler case of itself. The program can then perform one step of the solution, the step of calculating its result, by using the result for the simpler case and making a recursive call on itself to compute the result for that simpler case.

The program must, in the end, do just as much calculation as a direct solution; the calculations that are not made directly, but instead are obtained as the results of a recursive call, must be computed within that recursive call. The advantage of recursion lies in the simplification of the program code that is now possible. A recursive program can be written to make just one step toward the solution, using a recursive call to complete the solution. This is often much simpler than a program that aims for a direct solution, because such a program must solve the entire problem all at once.

Now let's consider an example in which we compute the greatest common divisor (gcd) of two non-negative integers m and n, that is, the largest integer that divides both. The algorithm is based on the observation that if a number divides both n and m **mod** n,[1] then it must also divide m. Thus, to find the gcd of m and n, we again invoke gcd on n and m **mod** n. Because the remainder is always smaller than the number we're dividing by, and because at each invocation we are dividing by the remainder from the enclosing invocation, the remainder will eventually become zero and the recursion will terminate.

```
(* This is a recursive function to find the gcd. *)
function gcd(m, n: nonnegint): nonnegint;
begin
  if (m = 0) and (n = 0) then
    writeln('gcd(0,0) is undefined.')
  else if n = 0 then
    gcd := m
  else
    gcd := gcd(n, m mod n)
end;
```

---

[1]Reminder: m **mod** n is the remainder of the division of m by n.

Figure 7.1 illustrates what happens when we call this function for, say, m = 4 and n = 6.

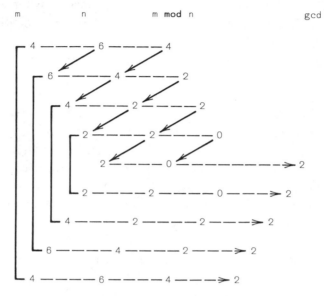

Figure 7.1 Recursive calls of gcd.

▶ Because m = 4 and n = 6 are both different from 0, the **else** part of the code is executed and gcd is called (notice that the routine calls itself) with 6 and m **mod** n = 4 **mod** 6 = 4 as the parameters.

▶▶ Because the new m and n for the recursive call are both different from 0, the **else** is executed again and gcd is called with the parameters 4 and m **mod** n = 6 **mod** 4 = 2.

▶▶▶ Because the new m and n are again both different from 0, the **else** is executed once again and gcd is called with the parameters 2 and m **mod** n = 2 **mod** 4 = 2.

▶▶▶▶ Because the new m and n are again both different from 0, the **else** is executed yet again and gcd is called with the parameters 2 and m **mod** n = 2 **mod** 2 = 0.

▶▶▶▶▶ Because m is different from 0 and n = 0, the **else if** portion of the code is executed, resulting in gcd (2,0) = 2.

►►►► The value 2 is then passed back to the previous level of the recursion, resulting in gcd (2,2) = 2.

►►► It is then passed back to the next previous recursive level, resulting in gcd (4,2) = 2.

►► It is then passed back again, resulting in gcd (6,4) = 2.

► Finally, the value 2 is passed back to the outermost level of the recursion, resulting in gcd (4,6) = 2.

To make sure that you understand how this works, step through another test case on your own. For example, try m = 17 and n = 10 and see if you get gcd (17, 10) = 1, as the result.

Instead of writing a recursive function to find the gcd, we could have written the following iterative function. Notice that the iterative version contains a termination condition in the while loop. The recursive version, on the other hand, does not contain a while loop (for recursion is used instead of iteration), but a similar termination condition is expressed in the if clause of the recursive version.

```
(* This is an iterative function to find the gcd. *)
function gcd(m, n: nonnegint): nonnegint;
var
   t: nonnegint;
begin
   if (m = 0) and (n = 0) then
      writeln('gcd(0,0) is undefined.')
   else
      begin
         while n <> 0 do
            begin
               t := m mod n;
               m := n;
               n := t
            end;
         gcd := m
      end
end;
```

In this case, to evaluate the gcd of 4 and 6, we have just a single function call, gcd(4,6); however, a loop is used to compute the gcd. Again, we have gcd(4,6) = 2 as the result.

Now let's consider a recursive procedure that accepts an integer in decimal form and prints it in binary form.

```
(* This procedure prints the binary *)
(* equivalent of an integer given    *)
(* in decimal form.                   *)

procedure converttobinary(n: nonnegint);
begin
   if n = 0 then
      write('the binary form is ')
   else
      begin
         converttobinary(n div 2);
         write(n mod 2 : 1)
      end
end;
```

Figure 7.2 illustrates what happens when, for example, n = 6.

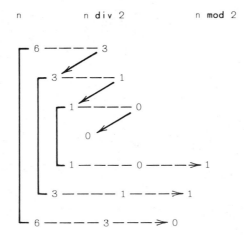

Figure 7.2 Recursive calls of converttobinary.

▶ Because the initial value of n is 6, the **else** portion of the code is executed, and converttobinary is called (notice the routine calls itself) with n **div** 2 = 6 **div** 2 = 3 as the parameter.

▶▶ Because the new n for the recursive call is 3, the **else** is executed, and converttobinary is called again but now with the parameter n **div** 2 = 3 **div** 2 = 1.

▶▶▶ Because the n for the recursive call is now 1, the **else** is executed again, and converttobinary is called with the parameter n **div** 2 = 1 **div** 2 = 0.

▶▶▶▶ Because n is now 0, the **if** portion of the code is finally executed, and the write statement prints "the binary form is. "

▶▶▶ Control then passes back to the previous level of the recursion, where n = 1, and the write statement prints n **mod** 2 = 1 **mod** 2 = 1.

▶▶ Control then passes back to the previous level, where n = 3 Because n **mod** 2 = 3 **mod** 2 = 1, the write statement prints another 1 (to the right of the first 1 that it printed).

▶ Finally, control passes back to the original level, where n = 6, and the write statement prints n **mod** 2 = 6 **mod** 2 = 0.

In summary, the procedure prints

110

which is 6 in binary. Run through another test case on your own. Try n = 8, and see if you get

1000.

56 With recursion, a problem solves itself.

Recursion fits naturally into a top-down, stepwise refinement approach to problem solving. In this approach a problem is split up into subproblems, with the idea that the subproblems will be easier to solve than the original problem. Each of the subproblems is, in turn, split up into still simpler subproblems, and so on, down to the simplest case. If a subproblem turns out to be similar to the original problem, differing only in that it is smaller in scale, then the problem is naturally recursive and a recursive algorithm might be written to solve the problem.

The first step in developing a recursive algorithm is to identify one or more simple cases of the problem that can be solved directly. The next step is to find a method of solving a complex case in terms of a simpler case. Often, the size of the problem is reduced by one or is cut in half. Eventually, however, the complex case must reduce to one or more simple nonrecursive cases.

To really understand recursion, it is best not to look down into the recursion and try to unwind the various levels. The human mind is not built to cope with this. Rather, you should treat the recursive call as you would a call to any other routine. Think of a recursive call as a call to some other routine that does the same thing as the one in question.

Let's suppose that we have an array a, in which the elements are sorted in increasing order, that is, $a[i] \le a[i+1]$, where $1 \le i < n$. We want to search the array a for a particular element k, called the key. The method that we employ is called binary search. If the key is not the middle element of the array, the search proceeds by dividing the problem into two subproblems: (1) Search the left subarray, and (2) search the right subarray. The process is repeated on the left and right subarrays and continues until either the key is found or a subarray with one or no elements remains (see Fig. 7.3).

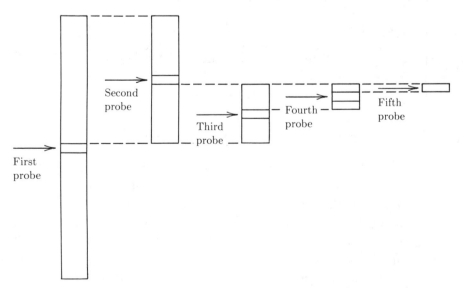

Figure 7.3 Probes in a binary search.

To solve the problem using this method, we write the following recursive function, which returns the subscript of the array element that matches the key k, if the key is found, and returns 0, otherwise.

```
(* This function searches an array a for a key k  *)
(* using the method of binary search.  It returns *)
(* the subscript, or index, of the array element  *)
(* that matches the key, if the key is found, and *)
(* returns 0, otherwise.                          *)
function indexfound(var a: posintarray; k: posint;
                     low, high: index): index;
var
  midpoint: index;
begin
  if low > high then
    indexfound := 0
  else
    begin
      midpoint := (low + high) div 2;
      if k < a[midpoint] then
        indexfound := indexfound(a,k,low,midpoint-1)
      else if k > a[midpoint] then
        indexfound := indexfound(a,k,midpoint+1,high)
      else
        indexfound := midpoint
    end
end;
```

In the examples considered thus far, a procedure or function is recursive because it calls itself directly. In indirect or mutual recursion, a procedure or function calls another, which calls another ... which calls the first. The simplest form of this involves two procedures or functions: A and B such that A calls B and B calls A.

Let's now consider an example of mutual recursion that has application in compiler design. The usual notation for algebraic expressions, in which the operators are written between the operands, is called infix notation. Another notation for algebraic expressions is reverse Polish, or postfix, notation in which the operators are written after the operands.

In an infix expression without parentheses, exponentiation (here denoted by $) is done before multiplication or division, and multiplication or division is done before addition or subtraction. These operations are done from left to right, with the exception of consecutive exponentiations, which are done from right to left. If parentheses are included, the operations in parentheses are done first.

Postfix expressions are generally simpler for computers than their corresponding infix equivalents, because the operations are performed in the order of the operators from left to right and parentheses can be omitted. Here are a few examples of algebraic expressions written in infix and postfix form:

infix	postfix
a * b + c	a b * c +
a * (b + c)	a b c + *
a / b $ c * d	a b c $ / d *
a + b $ c $ d * e	a b c d $ $ e * +
a + ((b + c) - d) * e	a b c + d - e * +

The conversion from infix to postfix form lends itself to recursion because the very definition of an infix expression is recursive.

- An expression is a term or an expression, followed by + or -, followed by a term.

- A term is a factor or a term, followed by * or /, followed by a factor.

- A factor is an item or an item followed by $, followed by a factor.

- An item is an expression enclosed in parentheses or a letter.

We now give a procedure that uses mutual recursion to convert an expression from infix to postfix form. We have the five procedures: expression, term, factor, item, and letter. Each of the four procedures, expression, term, factor, and letter, takes a character from the infix expression, which has been input by the user, and writes a character to the terminal. The procedure item reads parentheses from the infix expression but does not write them out. The procedures are mutually recursive in that expression calls term, which calls factor, which calls item (or factor), which calls expression (or letter).

Notice the use of **forward** in the declaration of the procedure expression. Pascal requires that a procedure or function be declared before it is used, but in a mutually recursive situation this is not possible. Pascal provides a **forward** reference to permit mutual recursion. In a **forward** reference, the procedure or function heading is given, including the parameters (if any) along with their types. When the procedure or function is declared later in the program, only the procedure or function name appears.

```
(* This program converts expressions from infix to *)
(* postfix form.  It uses the mutually recursive    *)
(* procedures expression, term, factor, item, and   *)
(* letter.  The end of an infix expression is       *)
(* indicated by a semicolon.  The program contains *)
(* a nonlocal goto, which standard Pascal accepts. *)
(* If your system does not accept it, comment out  *)
(* the label and goto, and print the additional    *)
(* message 'This is junk!' in the error routine.   *)

program convertinfixtopostfix(input, output);
label 1;
var
   ch: char;

(* When an error is detected, this procedure prints *)
(* an error message and returns to the main program. *)

procedure error;
begin
   writeln;
   writeln('Invalid expression. ',
           'Enter another expression.');
   writeln('No spaces between operators and operands,');
   writeln('one letter operands, $ for exponentiation.');
   goto 1
end;

procedure expression;
forward;
```

```
procedure letter;
var
   ch1: char;
begin
   read(ch1);
   if ch1 in ['a'..'z'] then
     write(ch1)        (* Write out the letter. *)
   else
     error
end;
procedure item;
var
   ch2: char;
begin
   if input↑ = '(' then
     begin
       read(ch2);      (* Skip past (. *)
       expression;     (*Write expression in postfix form.*)
       read(ch2);      (* Skip past ). *)
       if ch2 <> ')' then
          error
     end
   else
     letter            (* Write letter in postfix form. *)
end;
procedure factor;
var
   ch3: char;
begin
   item;               (* Write item in postfix form. *)
   if input↑ = '$' then
     begin
       read(ch3);      (* Save $. Advance to next char. *)
       factor;         (* Write factor in postfix form. *)
       write(ch3);     (* Write out $. *)
     end
end;
```

```
procedure term;
var
  ch4: char;
begin
  factor;            (* Write factor in postfix form. *)
  while (input↑ = '*') or (input↑ = '/') do
    begin
      read(ch4);     (*Save * or /. Advance to next char.*)
      factor;        (* Write factor in postfix form. *)
      write(ch4)     (* Write out * or /. *)
    end
end;

(* The procedure expression is called in the main *)
(* program.  It calls the procedure term, which   *)
(* calls factor, which calls item (or factor),    *)
(* which calls expression (or letter).            *)

procedure expression;
var
  ch5: char;
begin
  if input↑ <> ';' then
    begin
      term;          (* Write term in postfix form. *)
      while (input↑ = '+') or (input↑ = '-') do
        begin
          read(ch5); (*Save + or -. Advance to next char.*)
          term;      (* Write term in postfix form. *)
          write(ch5) (* Write out + or -. *)
        end
    end
  else
    begin
      read(ch5);     (* Save ;. Advance to end of line. *)
      writeln(ch5)   (* Write out ;. *)
    end
end;
```

```
begin (* Convertinfixtopostfix *)
  writeln('Enter an expression.');
  writeln('No spaces between operators and operands,');
  writeln('one letter operands, $ for exponentiation.');
  while not eof do
    begin
      while not eoln do
        expression;
      writeln('Enter another expression.');
1:    readln
    end
end.
```

As you can see from this example, when we're designing recursive procedures and functions, we don't worry about the details of the recursion or wind ourselves down into the depths of the recursion. Rather, we stay above it all and think of recursion simply in terms of one procedure or function calling another and the task that the procedure or function performs.

57 Each step is simpler than before; eventually there must be no more.

To be correct, a recursive routine must not generate an infinite sequence of calls to itself, for then it will not terminate. Thus, for at least one set of parameters, a recursive procedure or function must be defined in terms that do not involve itself. In other words, there must be a way out of the sequence of recursive calls.

Whenever a routine recurs, it must be with a simpler subproblem. If the routine recurs with an equally hard (or harder) problem, the recursion could go on forever. Furthermore, the routine must solve the simplest problems itself, without resorting to recursion. Problems cannot be simplified indefinitely. Sooner or later, real work must be done.

In writing a recursive routine, it's best to provide the termination condition first. For example, the founder of the new start-up company, Let's Play Games, Inc., wants to know how big his company will be after several years of compounded growth. The problem is one of computing

a^n, where a is a nonzero real number (the rate of growth) and n is a non-negative integer (the number of years). This problem can be solved very naturally by using recursion. To compute a^n, we first consider the termination case $n = 0$. In this case, $a^n = 1$, and we're done. If n is a positive even integer, then

$$a^n = (a^2)^{n \, \mathbf{div} \, 2}$$

whereas if n is odd, then

$$a^n = a * (a^2)^{n \, \mathbf{div} \, 2}$$

Thus, the problem of computing a^n can be reduced to a simpler problem, one with exponent half the size, continuing until the base case $n = 0$ is reached, at which point the recursion terminates.

```
function power(a: real; n: nonnegint): real;
begin
   if n = 0 then
      power := 1.0
   else if odd(n) then
      power := a * power(a*a, n div 2)
   else
      power := power(a*a, n div 2)
end;
```

Now, as a programmer for Let's Play Games, Inc., you are assigned to write a program for a video game in which a mouse tries to find a path through a maze. The maze is set up as an array of blanks and x's, with a border of x's around the outside (the x's correspond to brick walls through which the mouse cannot pass). For example,

```
X X X X X X X X X X X X X X X X X X X X X X X X X X X X X X X X
X X X X     X X X X X X X X X X X X X X X X X X X X X X X X X
X                                      X X X         X
X            X X X X X X X X X X X X X X     X X X       X
X                        X X X X X X                     X
X           X X X X X            X X X     X X X X X X X X X X
X           X X X X X X X X          X X X               X
X               X X X X X X X X X X X X X       X X X       X
X           X X X X X X X X X X X X X                 X X X   X
X                                        X X X             X
X X X X X X X X X X X X X X X         X X X X X X X X         X
X                                  X X X                 X
X X X X X X X X X X X X X X X X X X X X X X X X X         X X X X
X X X X X X X X X X X X X X X X X X X X X X X X X X X X X X X X
```

The coordinates of the starting position and finishing position are given. You write the following recursive procedure, which enables the mouse to find a path through the maze from the starting position to the finishing position.

```pascal
type
  mazeindex = 1..50;
  mazetype = array[mazeindex,mazeindex] of char;
  direction = (north,east,south,west);
  pathindex = 0..1200;
  position = record
                row, column: mazeindex
             end;
  pathtype = array[pathindex] of position;
var
  start, finish, current: position;
  step: pathindex;
  reached: boolean;
  maze: mazetype;
  path: pathtype;

(* Pathfinder is a recursive procedure that enables *)
(* a mouse to find a path through a maze from the   *)
(* current position to the finish.  The mouse       *)
(* backtracks upon encountering a brick wall or     *)
(* a cell that has already been visited.            *)
procedure pathfinder(current, finish: position;
                     var reached: boolean);
var
  dir: direction;
  next: position;

    (* Choosenextdirection computes the indices   *)
    (* of the next cell to be visited, proceeding *)
    (* in a clockwise direction.                  *)
    procedure choosenextdirection(var dir: direction;
            current: position; var next: position);
```

```
    begin (* Choosenextdirection *)
      next := current;
      if dir = west
      then
        dir := north
      else
        dir := succ(dir);
      case dir of
        north: next.column := current.column + 1;
        east : next.row := current.row + 1;
        south: next.column := current.column - 1;
        west : next.row := current.row - 1
      end
    end; (* Choosenextdirection *)

begin (* Pathfinder *)
 if (current.row = finish.row) and
    (current.column = finish.column) then
    reached := true
 else if (maze[current.row,current.column] = 'x') or
         (maze[current.row,current.column] = 'v') then
         reached := false
 else
   begin
     maze[current.row,current.column] := 'v';
     dir := west;
     repeat
       choosenextdirection(dir, current, next);
       step := step + 1;
       path[step].row := next.row;
       path[step].column := next.column;
       pathfinder(next, finish, reached);
       if not reached then
         step := step - 1
     until reached or (dir = west)
   end
end; (* Pathfinder *)
```

If the mouse hits a brick wall, it backtracks to the previous cell and tries another direction (north, east, south, west, in that order). If the mouse has already visited a cell, it does not want to visit that cell again; otherwise, it will go around in circles and get itself into an infinite loop. So at each cell it visits, the mouse leaves its mark (a "v" for visited), and it backtracks if it encounters the cell again. Thus, the recursion terminates if the finishing position is reached, and the mouse backtracks if it hits a wall or encounters a cell that it has already visited. In the main program, step is initialized to zero and pathfinder is called with start and reached. The array path contains the coordinates of the cells along the path.

The algorithm used above is an example from a class of algorithms known as backtracking algorithms, which are often expressed recursively. Although the algorithm is somewhat subtle, it illustrates the point that you must make sure that your recursions terminate.

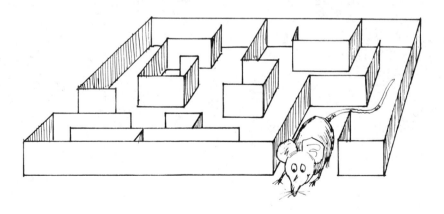

58 Local values! A new version for every level of recursion!

Each time a recursive procedure or function calls itself, a new set of storage locations must be allocated for all local variables, value parameters, temporary expressions, and the return address associated with that call. When control is returned to a point in a previous call, the most recent allocation of these variables is freed and the previous copy is reactivated.

The only local variables accessible are those of the most recent procedure call. Although they have the same names as those local to the previous call of the procedure, their values are distinct. Similarly, the value parameters accessible at different levels of the recursion are distinct. Remember, each level of recursion has its own copies of local variables and value parameters.

However, when global (i.e., nonlocal) variables are used in recursive procedures or functions, there is only one copy of each global variable, and this one instance is shared by all levels of the recursion. The same is true of reference (or **var**) parameters. Remember, if a global variable or reference parameter is altered, it is altered at all levels of the recursion.

Let's now consider an algorithm, called merge sort, for sorting an array. The idea is naturally recursive and very simple. We divide the array into two halves, sort each half, and then merge the two halves together. Each half is sorted, using this same procedure. If, however, the halves each contain one or zero elements, then they are already sorted and there is nothing more to do but to merge them together.

```
(* Mergesort splits a section of an array   *)
(* indexed from i to j into two halves and   *)
(* calls itself recursively for each half.   *)
(* When the halves are sorted, they are      *)
(* merged together.                          *)
procedure mergesort(var a: aarray; i, j: index);
var
   k: index;
begin
   if i < j then
      begin
         k := (i + j) div 2;
         mergesort(a,i,k);
         mergesort(a,k+1,j);
         merge(a,i,k,k+1,j)
      end
end;
```

The procedure mergesort calls the procedure merge, which can also be written as a recursive procedure. The procedure merge starts with two sections of the array, i to j and k to l. Each section is already sorted, but the two sections need not be contiguous, that is, right next to one another. The procedure merges them into one contiguous section, from i+k−j−1 to l. It does this by selecting either a[i] or a[k] as the least element and then calling itself recursively to merge the remaining elements (see Fig. 7.4).

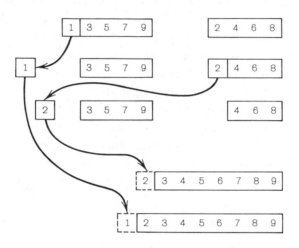

Figure 7.4 Merge.

If i > j, the left subarray is empty, and any elements still remaining in the right subarray are already correctly positioned; and so the recursion terminates. Otherwise, there are three subcases to consider, each of which requires merging. If k > l, the right subarray is empty, and therefore the least element must be in the left subarray. If not, then both subarrays are not empty, and either the least element is in the left subarray or it is in the right subarray.

Note that a different local (that is, temporary) variable t is used to record the least element at each level of the recursion. When the recursion terminates, all of the elements (except those already positioned correctly at the end of the right subarray) are held in these temporary variables, one at each level. As the recursion unwinds, each of the elements is placed in its proper place in the array (starting at the back end) before the procedure at that level exits and the temporary variable disappears.

```
(* Merge is a recursive procedure that merges *)
(* two sections of an array from i to j and   *)
(* from k to l that have already been sorted. *)
procedure merge(var a: aarray; i, j, k, l: index);
var
   t: aitem;
begin
   if i <= j then
     if k > l then
       begin
         t := a[i];
         merge(a,i+1,j,k,l);
         a[i+k-j-1] := t
       end
     else if a[i] <= a[k] then
       begin
         t := a[i];
         merge(a,i+1,j,k,l);
         a[i+k-j-1] := t
       end
     else
       begin
         t := a[k];
         merge(a,i,j,k+1,l);
         a[i+k-j-1] := t
       end
end;
```

59 Before you say recursion's fine, count the cost in space and time.

Each recursive call requires the saving of an additional set of local variables, value parameters, and return addresses. Thus, a recursive algorithm is potentially much more expensive in its use of memory than a simple iterative algorithm. To reduce the amount of storage space used in recursion, it's important to ensure that large structures, such as arrays or records, are passed as reference (or **var**) parameters; otherwise, copies will be made for each level of the recursion.

Besides the additional memory required for recursive procedures and functions, we must beware of excessive execution times, too. For example, consider the function $f(n) = 2^n$. This can be written recursively, as follows:

```
(* This function computes the nth power *)
(* of 2 recursively.                    *)

function twotothe(n: nonnegint): posint;
begin
   if n = 0 then
      twotothe := 1
   else
      twotothe := twotothe(n-1) + twotothe(n-1)
end;
```

If n = 5, for example, then twotothe(5) calls twotothe(4) twice, each of these call twotothe(3) twice, these in turn call twotothe(2) twice, which call twotothe(1) twice, which finally calls twotothe(0). Thus, the total number of calls of the function twotothe is

$$1 + 2 + 4 + 8 + 16 + 32 = 63 = 2^6 - 1.$$

If n = 10, the total number of function calls is

$$1 + 2 + \ldots + 2^{10} = 2^{11} - 1 = 2047.$$

More generally, in the evaluation of twotothe(n), the depth of the recursion is only n, but the total number of function calls is $2^{n+1} - 1$, which grows very fast as n gets large. Clearly, one would not want to evaluate 2^n in this way.

As a second example, let's consider Pascal's triangle. Each number in the triangle is the sum of two numbers in the row above it, except for the 1's along the edges.

$$1$$
$$1 \quad 1$$
$$1 \quad 2 \quad 1$$
$$1 \quad 3 \quad 3 \quad 1$$
$$1 \quad 4 \quad 6 \quad 4 \quad 1$$
$$1 \quad 5 \quad 10 \quad 10 \quad 5 \quad 1$$

Like baking soda, Pascal's triangle has many uses. One of the many is that it gives the coefficients of the terms in the expansion of $(a + b)^n$. For example,

$$(a + b)^2 = 1a^2 + 2ab + 1b^2$$

and

$$(a + b)^3 = 1a^3 + 3a^2 + 3ab^2 + 1.$$

These are referred to as the binomial coefficients and are usually denoted by $\binom{n}{k}$. This is read "n choose k" because it gives us the number of ways of choosing k things out of n things. For example, if we want to find how many ways a software development team of five can be chosen from a group of eight programmers, the answer is eight choose five, that is $\binom{8}{5} = 56$. For more information, sign up for a course on discrete mathematics or combinatorics.

Getting back to Pascal's triangle, $\binom{n}{k}$ is the kth number in the nth row of the triangle, where the top row is the 0th row and the left-most number in each row is the 0th number. For example, in the second row we have $\binom{2}{0} = 1$, $\binom{2}{1} = 2$, and $\binom{2}{2} = 1$. In terms of this notation, we can see from the triangle that

$$\binom{n}{k} = \begin{cases} 1 & \text{if } k = 0 \text{ or } k = n \\ \binom{n-1}{k-1} + \binom{n-1}{k} & \text{if } 0 < k < n \end{cases}$$

Once we see this relation, it's easy to write a recursive function in Pascal to compute these numbers.

```
(* This function computes the binomial coefficient, *)
(* n choose k, using its recursive definition.      *)

function bincoef(n, k: nonnegint): nonnegint;
begin
   if (k = 0) or (k = n) then
      bincoef := 1
   else
      bincoef := bincoef(n-1,k-1) + bincoef(n-1,k)
end;
```

Like the twotothe function, this function is very inefficient because each evaluation of bincoef(n,k) for $k \neq 0$ and $k \neq n$ requires two further evaluations, and the same evaluations are performed over and over again. Moreover, because the binomial coefficients can also be defined by

$$\binom{n}{k} = \frac{n!}{k!(n-k)!}$$

we can write a nonrecursive function that is much more efficient. First, we cancel the larger of $k!$ and $(n-k)!$ from the numerator and denominator.

```
(* This function computes the binomial coefficient, *)
(* n choose k, iteratively using its definition in   *)
(* terms of factorials.  The user-defined functions  *)
(* max and min are called by this function.          *)

function bincoef(n, k: nonnegint): nonnegint;
var
   numerator, denominator, i, m: nonnegint;
begin
   (* Factor the maximum of k! and (n-k)! *)
   (* out of the numerator.               *)
   m := max(k, n-k);
   numerator := n;
   for i := n-1 downto m+1 do
      numerator := numerator * i;
```

```
(* Make the denominator the minimum of *)
(* k! and (n-k)!.                       *)
m := min(k, n-k);
denominator := m;
for i := m-1 downto 1 do
  denominator := denominator * i;

(* Find n choose k by dividing the      *)
(* numerator by the denominator.        *)
  bincoef := numerator div denominator
end;
```

Usually, it's possible to convert a recursive procedure or function into an iterative one. If you use the same basic algorithm, you will probably realize only a twofold or threefold gain in efficiency. If space or time is really a problem, this is not enough. To obtain more significant gains (10-fold or more), you must use a different iterative algorithm, as we have done in the example above.

In summary, recursion should not be used when there is an equally good and obvious iterative solution. However, when the underlying algorithm is naturally recursive, then, subject to memory and time requirements, recursion can be used in the interests of clarity, conciseness, and elegance.

Problems and Projects

1. Given the recursive gcd function in Proverb 55, make a table of the values of the variables for each recursive call when the function is called initially for m = 29 and n = 83.

2. Get a copy of *Godel, Escher, Bach: An Eternal Golden Braid* by Douglas R. Hofstadter (Basic Books: New York, 1979), and read Chapter V: "Recursive Structures and Processes." Write a summary of what you have learned.

3. A palindrome is a string that reads the same forward and backward when punctuation marks, blanks, and capitalization are ignored. For example,

> Madam, I'm Adam.
> A man, a plan, a canal, Panama.
> Too hot to hoot.

are palindromes. Write a recursive procedure that takes a string and determines whether or not the string is a palindrome. You may assume that the string ends in a period. Rewrite the procedure, using iteration. How do the structures of the two procedures compare?

4. Write a recursive function to find a solution to an equation, $f(x) = 0$, using the interval bisection method described in Proverb 10. Why is recursion more appropriate than iteration for the interval bisection method? Which is more efficient?

5. Mr. Liker of the Fly-by-Night Dating Service (see Proverb 17) has noticed that his current programs do not yield the maximum number of acceptable dating matches. Consider the situation depicted below with the possible matches indicated.

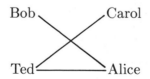

By choosing to match Ted and Alice, the program finds only one match and misses the alternative of Bob/Alice and Ted/Carol, which provides two matches.

Mr. Liker needs a new program, the first phase of which constructs a list of matches for each female and male. The second phase, then, has to choose matches from this list so as to maximize the number of matches while limiting each female and male to a single match.

The basic structure of the second phase is a recursive procedure that consists of the following steps: (a) For the first female on the list, consider in turn each of her matches from the list and also the case in which she is matched to nobody, and (b) invoke the procedure recursively to find the maximum number of matches remaining, using a list from which all references to the female or to her matching male (if any) have been removed.

Write the recursive procedure described above to find the maximum number of dating matches for Fly-by-Night. Discuss the termination condition of your procedure and contrast it to other possible termination conditions.

6. Besides infix and postfix notation, a third notation used in writing algebraic expressions is prefix notation. In prefix notation, the operators are written before the operands. Here are some infix expressions and their corresponding prefix equivalents.

infix	prefix
a * b + c	+ * a b c
a * (b + c)	* a + b c
a / b $ c * d	* / a $ b c d
a + b $ c $ d * e	+ a * $ b $ c d e
a + ((b + c) - d) * e	+ a * - + b c d e

Write a Pascal program that uses mutual recursion to convert an expression from infix to prefix form. See the example for converting infix to postfix form in Proverb 56.

7. As a systems programmer for Monster Multiprogramming Machines, you are given the assignment of writing a program to allocate space on a disk. The file is typically longer than any of the free areas on the disk. You must allocate space for the file out of the free areas available with as little waste as possible. Use a backtracking algorithm in which you allocate one of the areas and then allocate space for the rest of the file using recursion.

To implement the algorithm, set up an array of records, each of which contains a length and a flag to indicate whether the area is allocated. Search down the array for free (unallocated) areas, and consider each of the free areas in turn. If the length of a free area is greater than or equal to the remaining space required by the file, record the difference as a waste and terminate the recursion. If the length of the free area is less than the amount of space, subtract the length from the space needed by the file and mark the area as having been used and call the procedure recursively. You may pass the array either as a value parameter or as a reference parameter to your procedure. But if you pass the array as a reference parameter, then, after marking an area as having been used and calling the procedure recursively, you must unmark the area.

8. As distributor of the Florida Flowering Flyswatter, a bug-devouring house plant, Flying Flo must make regular visits to each of the cities in which her retail dealers are located. Thus, an important question is: In what order should the cities be visited so as to minimize her total round-trip distance? This problem is known as the traveling salesman problem, or, in the case of Flo, the traveling saleswoman problem.

    To solve this problem you may assume the existence of a function that gives the distance between any pair of cities; in this example, we will implement the function as a square array indexed by the cities. You will also need a one-dimensional array of cities that records whether or not a city has been visited. In addition, you will need a one-dimensional array of cities that represents the appropriate order in which to visit the cities.

    Once you have set up these arrays, write a recursive procedure that takes as input the array of distances and returns an array of cities in the order in which they should be visited to minimize the round-trip distance. At each stage of the recursion, the array of cities indicates which cities have already been visited. Select each of the other cities as a possible next city to visit by calling the procedure recursively.

The procedure returns with its best distance for visiting the remaining cities and the order in which to visit them. Add this distance to the distance to the selected city. Then choose the best total distance and append the selected city to the list of cities returned by that recursive call to generate your result. You may pass the array either as a value parameter or as a reference parameter to your procedure. But if you pass the array as a reference parameter, after marking a city as having been visited and calling the procedure recursively, you must unmark the city.

When you have finished writing the procedure, discuss how the termination condition for your recursion could be modified to eliminate obviously inappropriate routes as early as possible.

8
Dynamic
Storage Allocation

In many computer applications, there are changes not only in the data but also in the amount of data during execution of a program. To accommodate this varying amount of data, Pascal provides us with a mechanism for allocating storage dynamically. Memory space for dynamically allocated variables is allocated by specific statements within a program and remains available until it is disposed of by further statements in the program. In contrast, memory space for variables declared in a program block is static because space is provided as the block is entered and remains in use until the block is exited.

Dynamically allocated variables are often used to build linked lists. Each dynamic variable in a linked list is a record that contains a link to the next record in the list. Thus, a linked list is a chain of records in which each record is linked to the next; from the first record in the chain, we can follow the links to gain access to all of the others.

Although static structures, like arrays, are very useful in simple situations, dynamically allocated variables can be used in more complex applications. The techniques of artificial intelligence, for example, are largely based on dynamic structures.

In this chapter we consider the features of dynamically allocated variables, we address some subtle points and potential problems in their use, and we show you how to build linked lists and more complex dynamic structures. It's time for a change now, so let's think dynamic!

210

60 Be dynamic for flexibility.

In programming applications, we need to store data, but often we are not sure exactly how much data we will be storing. Therefore, we may not know how much memory space will be necessary. Furthermore, in some applications, space requirements may fluctuate while the program is running.

When we store data in an array, we are confined by the length that we have declared for the array. If we continue placing information into the array, we will eventually run out of space to store additional data. We can, of course, set aside a lot of extra space in the array, but that would be wasteful, and who knows how much we might need! Fortunately, Pascal provides us with a dynamic storage mechanism—the pointer—that enables us to build dynamic data structures in which we can store arbitrary amounts of data.

Dynamic data structures, such as linked lists, are particularly useful when structures change in size during the execution of a program, for example, when insertions and deletions are frequently done. If a sequence of data is represented in an array, insertions and deletions require shifting the sequence along the array. Unless the element to be inserted or deleted is near the end of the array, a large amount of data will have to be moved one position forward or backward. If, on the other hand, the sequence is constructed as a linked list, it is relatively easy to create a new component and insert it between two existing ones or to delete an existing component. What we must do is redirect the pointers, which is a lot faster than copying the array.

Let's consider the case of the No Doubt About It Insurance Company. Recently, this unquestionably solid company decided to computerize its list of clients. The programmer who designed the client address system used an array of records to store the several thousand names and addresses of the company's clients with the records ordered alphabetically by clients' names. Here is a pictorial representation of one very small portion of this array (records 300 and 301).

| 300 | Calamity, Chris | 1 Claim Ct. | Outoluck, OK |
| 301 | Clutz, Clyde | 5 Tripp Rd. | Banana Peel, TX |

The day after the new system was implemented on the company's central computer, the company's agent in Casualty, Colorado, signed up Cathy Catastrophe as a new client. In order to add Cathy's information to the new system, the several thousand records following the one for Chris Calamity had to be moved down in the array, just to make the following change:

300	Calamity, Chris	1 Claim Ct.	Outoluck, OK
301	Catastrophe, Cathy	9 Disaster Dr.	Casualty, CO
302	Clutz, Clyde	5 Tripp Rd.	Banana Peel, TX

The insurance company soon discovered that having to make such changes every day (and often several times a day) was not very efficient. So the company's programmer rewrote the program, using linked lists (Fig. 8.1).

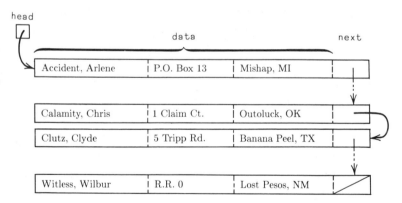

Figure 8.1 Linked list.

Note that the records now have two fields, one called data and one called next. There is also a variable, called head. The head and the next fields provide the links necessary to connect these records together into a list. As you can see, Arlene Accident is at the head of the list. Each of the next fields contains pointer information, which tells us where we can find the next item in the list. The last item in the list contains a special nil pointer in its next field, which tells us that we're at the end of the list. This is indicated by a diagonal in the diagram.

It was then very simple for the No Doubt About It Insurance Company to insert a client's record and yet maintain the alphabetical order. For example, to insert the record for Cathy Catastrophe, they simply put the data into a new node[1] and inserted the new node into the list, adjusting the pointers as necessary (Fig. 8.2).

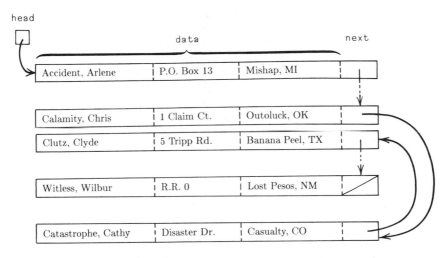

Figure 8.2 Newly inserted record.

Now that was relatively easy, wasn't it? There was no need to disturb any of the information in the data fields of the client records. Instead, just a few simple operations were necessary. (You'll read more about these operations in Proverb 63.)

In contrast to arrays with their static length and structure, dynamic data structures are certainly more flexible. However, arrays may be more appropriate for some applications, particularly when the amount of memory required is known in advance. Furthermore, arrays occupy less storage space because no pointers are required, and the components of an array can be accessed by means of subscripts, which is quicker than traversing[2] a linked list, until the desired component is found. Nevertheless, for flexibility, dynamic data structures are preferred.

---

[1]Node—a component in a linked list or other dynamic data structure.

[2]Traverse—to move along or through.

61 Pointers only point.

Dynamic storage locations, that is, dynamic variables, are referenced by the use of pointers. The value of a pointer is the address of the storage location it references. The data values in the storage location are accessed and can only be accessed indirectly through the pointer. Consider, for example, the following declaration:

```
type
    datatype = ...;
    nodeptr = ↑listitem;
    listitem = record
                    data: datatype;
                    next: nodeptr
               end;
var
    listhead, p, q: nodeptr;
```

If p is the pointer declared above, then the object to which it points, or the referenced variable as it is called, is denoted by p↑. The referenced variable p↑ is a record located at the address given in p. The record

p↑ has two fields, a data field and a pointer field, which are denoted by
p↑.data and p↑.next (see Fig. 8.3).

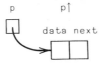

Figure 8.3 A pointer and its referenced variable.

It is very important to distinguish between the pointer and the object
to which it points. If a pointer variable appears without the ↑, the pointer
value itself (rather than the contents of the referenced storage location)
will be manipulated. Suppose, for example, that we have a situation such
as that in Fig. 8.4.

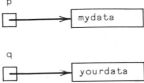

Figure 8.4 p and q point to different cells with different data.

The assignment

$$p := q$$

copies the contents of the pointer variable q into the pointer variable p.
Both pointers now point to the same storage location (Fig. 8.5).

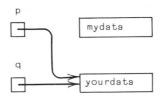

Figure 8.5 p and q point to the same cell.

On the other hand, the statement

$$p↑ := q↑$$

copies the contents of the referenced variable q↑ into the referenced variable p↑. In this case, the pointers are unchanged (each pointer points to a different location), but the value of p↑ has been altered, so that the two locations now contain the same value (Fig. 8.6).

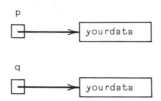

Figure 8.6 p and q point to different cells with the same data.

The declaration of a pointer variable p only allocates space for the variable; it does not assign it a value. Even if the compiler initializes it to **nil** (and some compilers do), it does not reference a storage location. Before a reference can be made, a storage location must be allocated, using the procedure new. Storage space that can be allocated dynamically is kept on an "available space list." The procedure call

new(p)

takes a block of storage from the available space list and assigns the address of that block to p. Alternatively, the value of some other pointer variable can be assigned to p, allowing p to be used to access a storage location allocated previously.

Remember, the declaration of the pointer variable p does not create an object to which p points, only the capability to do so. Creation of such an object is achieved using the standard procedure new.

62 To make it clear, point it out.

In the type declaration above, we built a pointer field into the record so that we could use it to link one record to another to form a linked list. In such a list each node can be accessed from the previous one. Thus, all that we need is a pointer to the first node to access any node in the list.

Consider the following function in which we step down, or traverse, a list looking for the last node. We introduce an extra pointer variable p to make it clear what we're doing. The pointer p progresses down the list until it reaches the last node, at which point p↑.next becomes nil.

```
(* This function returns a pointer to the last node *)
(* of the list pointed to by listhead.  If the list *)
(* is empty, it returns the nil pointer.            *)

function grabthetail(listhead: nodeptr): nodeptr;
var
   p: nodeptr;
begin
   p := listhead;
   if p <> nil then
     while p↑.next <> nil do
       p := p↑.next;
   grabthetail := p
end;
```

We could dispense with the pointer variable p and write the following function instead. However, when one sees listhead being changed in the statement listhead := listhead↑.next, or when one looks at the statement grabthetail := listhead, in which it appears that the tail is identified with the head, some uncertainty or confusion might arise.

```
(* This function returns a pointer to the last node *)
(* of the list pointed to by listhead.  If the list *)
(* is empty, it returns the nil pointer.            *)

function grabthetail(listhead: nodeptr): nodeptr;
begin
   if listhead <> nil then
     while listhead↑.next <> nil do
       listhead := listhead↑.next;
   grabthetail := listhead
end;
```

Although we don't recommend this second version of the function, it is correct. Do you understand why? The pointer listhead is passed as a value parameter, and thus a local copy of it is made, when the function is entered. This local copy is used for the traversal, whereas the corresponding pointer in the calling program remains unchanged. Because pointers require very little storage space, it's better to use an extra pointer declared as a local variable instead of a pointer passed as a value parameter. Not only do such pointers add to the clarity of your program but they minimize the possibility of error.

Another consideration, based on the storage space used by pointers, is that if you're dealing with pointers to objects which require a lot of space, such as arrays or records, and you're considering passing the object as a value parameter, you should pass the pointer instead. The storage space required by a pointer is usually quite small compared to that required by the object to which it points. In using pointers as parameters, be careful in your use of value and reference parameters.

- If you are passing a parameter into a procedure or function and its value is not changed, you should use a value parameter, as in

```
procedure printarecord(p: nodeptr);
begin
   (* Here we print the contents of p↑.data. *)
end;
```

- If you are assigning a new value to a pointer parameter for use by the calling code on exit, you must use a reference (or **var**) parameter, as in

```
procedure createarecord(var p: nodeptr);
var
   tempdata: datatype;
begin
   (* Here we read the data into tempdata. *)
   new(p);
   p↑.data := tempdata;
   p↑.next := nil
end;
```

- If you are modifying the fields of a record passed in as a parameter but do not make an assignment to the record pointer itself, you should use a value parameter. Even though the pointer is a value parameter, the changes to the fields of the record will be available to the calling program on exit, as in

```
procedure updatearecord(p: nodeptr);
var
   tempdata: datatype;
begin
   tempdata := p↑.data;
   (* Here we change the data in tempdata. *)
   p↑.data := tempdata
end;
```

63 A missing link has no successor.

When you are working with linked structures, you must be careful to retain access to each item of data, so that none is inadvertently lost. If all of the pointers to a data item are overwritten, there is no way to access it—in effect, the data item is lost.

During insertions and deletions, particular care must be taken to avoid losing contact with part of a linked structure. When these operations are performed, the order in which statements are executed is crucial, so be careful!

In your part-time position with Max's Mail Order Madhouse, a catalog mail order company, Max (the boss) assigns you the task of creating a mailing list into which data can be readily inserted and deleted. Within the company's computer system there already exists a file of records, one for each customer with his or her name, address, outstanding balance, and date of most recent purchase.

To carry out the assignment, you must first write a procedure to insert a new node into a list. This is done quite simply by creating a new node, directing the pointer of the new node to the new node's successor, and then redirecting the pointer in the new node's predecessor to the new node you have created.

```
(* This procedure inserts the node *)
(* pointed to by q after the node  *)
(* pointed to by p.                *)

procedure insertafter(p, q: nodeptr);
begin
  if p = nil then
    writeln('Insertafter was called ',
            'with a nil pointer.')
  else
    begin
      q↑.next := p↑.next;
      p↑.next := q
    end
end;
```

The scenarios before and during the execution of the procedure insertafter are shown in Fig. 8.7 and 8.8 on this page and the next.

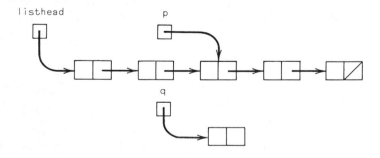

Figure 8.7 Prior to insertafter.

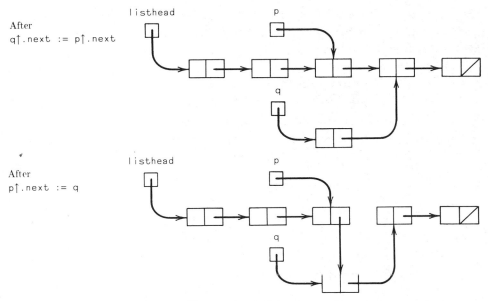

Figure 8.8 Execution of insertafter.

Notice what happens if we interchange the order of the statements used to link in the new node, that is, if we write, instead,

```
p↑.next := q;
q↑.next := p↑.next
```

Part of the original list is lost and what remains contains a loop—clearly not what we had intended (see Fig. 8.9).

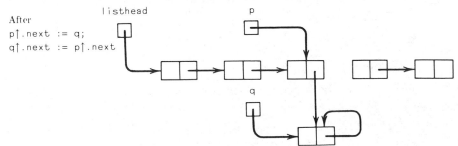

Figure 8.9 Incorrect order of insertion statements.

Once you have written the procedure for inserting a new node after a given node in a list, you can use it to build an entirely new list, as in the following procedure:

```
(* This procedure creates a list pointed to   *)
(* by listhead, by calling the procedure       *)
(* insertafter repeatedly.  It also calls the *)
(* function nomoredata and the procedures       *)
(* createarecord and insertafter.               *)
procedure createalist(var listhead: nodeptr);
var
  p, q: nodeptr;
begin
  if nomoredata then
    listhead := nil
  else
    begin
      (* Anchor the list. *)
      createarecord(listhead);

      (* Insert the remaining data. *)
      p := listhead;
      while not nomoredata do
        begin
          createarecord(q);
          insertafter(p,q);
          p := p↑.next (* Advance p to the new node. *)
        end
    end
end;
```

Notice that if there are no data, we set listhead to nil. The nil pointer is a special one that points to nothing; it is not the same as an undefined pointer. We also assign nil to the next field of each new node that we create, but this nil is overwritten when a new node is linked to it. When we are finished, only the very last node will have a nil in its next field. At the time a list is created, it's very important to mark the last node by storing **n i l** in its next field, so that on subsequent traversals you know when you're at the end of the list. When working with dynamic data structures, ask yourself if you have

- Kept a pointer to the first node in the list.

- Updated the pointers to the current and, perhaps, previous nodes.

- Set the next field of each node properly.

- Set the next field of the last node to **n i l**.

Dynamic data structures, such as the list created above, will disappear when execution of your program terminates. When you run your program again, the entire structure must be recreated. Thus, if you wish to use the same data again, these data should be written to a file. Note that only the data and not the pointers associated with them should be written to the file, because the values in the pointers are temporary addresses that will not be meaningful when the program is run again. (A sequential list structure, as in our example, is easily written out to a file and read back in again.) Note also that if you make insertions and deletions in a dynamic structure created from a file, you will probably want to rewrite the updated data back out to the file.

64 Pointer nil, data none.

Accessing the referenced variable of a pointer that is **n i l** will result in a run-time error. Your program will crash with an error message like

```
Reference through a nil pointer
```

or

```
Invalid pointer reference
```

Consider, for example, the following function that searches a list for the key data and returns a pointer to the first node in the list that contains that data.

```
(* This function searches a list for key data.    *)
(* It returns a pointer to the first node in      *)
(* the list that contains the key, if it exists,  *)
(* and nil otherwise.                             *)
function keypointer(listhead: nodeptr;
                       keydata: datatype): nodeptr;
var
   p: nodeptr;
begin
   p := listhead;
   while p↑.data <> keydata do
      p := p↑.next;
   keypointer := p
end;
```

If the list is empty, that is, if p = nil, then p↑ does not exist, and trying to access p↑.data in the condition of the while loop will cause a run-time error. Even if the list is not empty, a similar problem occurs if the key is not in the list. In this case, the list is traversed to the very end, p becomes nil, and when the condition of the while loop is checked, the program will crash because p↑.data cannot be accessed when p is nil.

If we replace the above loop condition with

```
while (p <> nil) and (p↑.data <> keydata) do
```

we may still have a problem, because most implementations of Pascal test both conditions even if the first is false. Again, in this case, when p = nil, p↑.data cannot be accessed, and the program will crash due to a run-time error.

A better way to write this function is to use a boolean variable and check for the end of the list, as follows:

```
(* This function searches a list for key data.   *)
(* It returns a pointer to the first node in      *)
(* the list that contains the key, if it exists,  *)
(* and nil otherwise.                             *)
function keypointer(listhead: nodeptr;
                    keydata: datatype): nodeptr;
var
  p: nodeptr;
  found: boolean;
begin
  p := listhead;
  found := false;
  while (p <> nil) and not found do
    if p↑.data = keydata then
      found := true
    else
      p := p↑.next;
  keypointer := p
end;
```

65 Useless data? Use dispose.

If you allocate dynamic storage locations without ever returning any to the available space list for possible reallocation, you will eventually run out of space and get a run-time error message, like

```
          Ran out of memory
```

or

```
          Workspace is full
```

Remember, a dynamic variable, created by calling new, remains in existence until it is disposed of or until execution of the program terminates. Its lifetime is not related to the block in which it is created or the block in which the pointer variables referencing it are declared.

The standard procedure dispose allows you to return dynamic variables no longer needed to the available space list, so that the space that they formerly occupied can be reused later on, if necessary. After you call dispose(p), p still exists, but it is undefined and doesn't reference any storage location. Thus, you must be very careful in using this procedure. You would not want to dispose of a referenced variable while it's still in use, and you cannot use such a variable once it's been disposed of.

The order in which you call dispose relative to other pointer manipulations is extremely important. In deletions from a linked list, for example, the pointer in the node's predecessor must be redirected to point to the node's successor before the dispose procedure is called; otherwise the successor will be lost and, along with it, the rest of the list.

Before sending out his new catalog, Max wants to delete customers from the mailing list who haven't made a purchase in a year. (He's worried about printing and mailing costs, as well as storage economy in his computer.) To carry out the task, the following procedure is written:

```
(* In this procedure, p points to a node in the  *)
(* mailing list.  The procedure deletes the node *)
(* following the node pointed to by p.  If p or  *)
(* p↑.next is nil, an error message is printed.  *)
procedure deleteafter(p: nodeptr;
                      var datadeleted: datatype);
var
   q: nodeptr;
begin
   if p <> nil then
     if  p↑.next <> nil then
       begin
         q := p↑.next;
         datadeleted := q↑.data;
         p↑.next := q↑.next;
         dispose(q)
       end
     else writeln('deleteafter was called ',
                  'but no successor.')
   else writeln('deleteafter was called ',
                'for a nil pointer.')
   end;
```

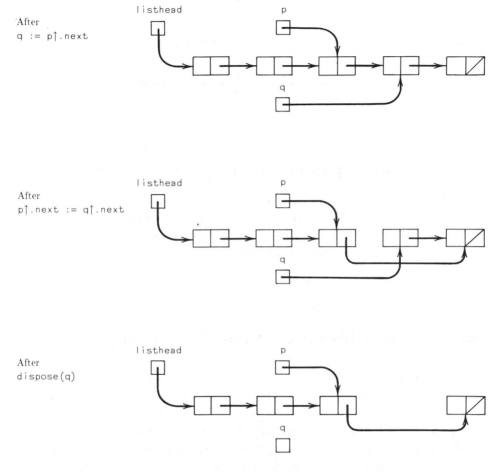

After
q := p↑.next

After
p↑.next := q↑.next

After
dispose(q)

Figure 8.10 Execution of deleteafter.

The effects of execution of this procedure are illustrated in Fig. 8.10 above. If the order of the deletion statements had been interchanged, that is, if the following had been written,

```
dispose(q) ;
p↑.next := q↑.next
```

then q would become undefined and q↑ (and hence q↑.next) would become inaccessible (see Fig. 8.11).

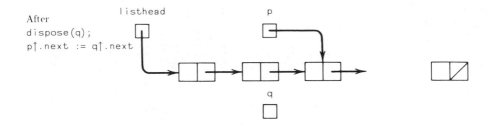

Figure 8.11 Incorrect order of deletion statements.

To maintain storage economy, it is the responsibility of the programmer to ensure that all referenced variables are disposed of when they are no longer needed and before the pointers to them are lost. If the pointer to a storage location is lost, there is no way to access it and no way to dispose of it.

66 Give special care to special cases.

When writing procedures or functions that manipulate dynamic data structures, it's a good idea to check the boundary cases. You must consider which special cases arise for the particular dynamic data structure you're using; there will be more special cases for some dynamic data structures than for others. In particular, if you're using singly linked lists,[3] as we have been doing, ask yourself: Will the procedure or function work

- If the list is empty?

- If the list has just one component?

- At the beginning of the list?

- At the end of the list?

---

[3]Singly linked list—a list whose nodes contain only one pointer. Such a list can be traversed in only one direction.

Now, let's consider an example. The following procedure is supposed to print the data in the nodes of a linked list. It calls the procedure printarecord, which we defined in Proverb 62.

```
procedure printalist(listhead: nodeptr);
var
   p: nodeptr;
begin
   p := listhead;
   while p↑.next <> nil do
      begin
         printarecord(p);
         p := p↑.next
      end
end;
```

There are several problems with this example. If the procedure is called with an empty list, a run-time error will occur because we're trying to access the next field of a record that doesn't exist. However, even if the list is not empty, there is still a problem—the data in the last node will not be printed! Convince yourself of this by drawing a diagram. The procedure should be modified as follows:

```
procedure printalist(listhead: nodeptr);
var
   p: nodeptr;
begin
   p := listhead;
   if p = nil then
      writeln('The list is empty.')
   else while p <> nil do
      begin
         printarecord(p);
         p := p↑.next
      end
end;
```

67 Keep your pointers straight to avoid a can of worms.

When you are dealing with lists that contain related information, it is important that you maintain consistency of these lists. If the lists share some of the same records, special care must be taken when manipulating the lists, particularly when doing insertions and deletions.

For example, Hacker's Scalpers, A Professional Partnership, keeps lists of individuals according to their current and prospective employers. To economize on storage space, they maintain a single record for each individual, which may occur in two lists: a current employer list and a prospective employer list. The employer lists are maintained as doubly linked (or two-way-linked) lists.[4] Thus,

```
type
    astring = array[1..30] of char;
    indivptr = ↑indivrec;
    ptrrec = record
                head, prev, next: indivptr
             end;
    indivrec = record
                  name, address: astring;
                  socsecno, phoneno: integer;
                  curr: ptrrec;
                  prosp: indivptr
               end;
var
    x, y, z: indivrec;
```

The record x would look like Fig. 8.12.

Figure 8.12 Record with several pointer fields.

---

[4]Doubly linked list—a list in which each node has a pointer both to its successor and to its predecessor.

In carrying out their head-hunting activities, it is important that Hacker's Scalpers keep their lists properly organized so that when someone moves from one company to another, the company has an accurate view of the employment picture.

If, for example, individual X is currently working for company A and is hoping to move to company B, X would appear on the current employees list of company A and on the prospective employees list of company B. If X lands the job at company B, he or she must be removed from each of these lists and must be inserted on the current employees list of company B. In carrying out these operations, we must be very careful to do them in the correct order.

```
(* This procedure deletes a record x    *)
(* from the current employer's list      *)
(* and inserts it into the prospective *)
(* employer's list.  It then sets the    *)
(* pointer to the prospective employer *)
(* to nil.                               *)

procedure deleteandinsert(var x: indivrec);
begin
   delete(x.curr);
   insert(x.prosp, x.curr);
   x.prosp := nil
end;
```

We use the pointer to the prospective employer to update the current employer before we delete the prospective employer. Thus, we have the scenario shown in Fig. 8.13 and 8.14 before and during execution of the procedure deleteandinsert. Portions of Hacker's Scalpers lists before execution of deleteandinsert and after delete are shown on p. 232. The lists after insert are shown on p. 233.

As this example illustrates, when you are manipulating several lists with related information, you must be very careful to maintain consistent information in the lists; otherwise, you will not be able to extract the appropriate information when you need it, or the results you get will be totally meaningless.

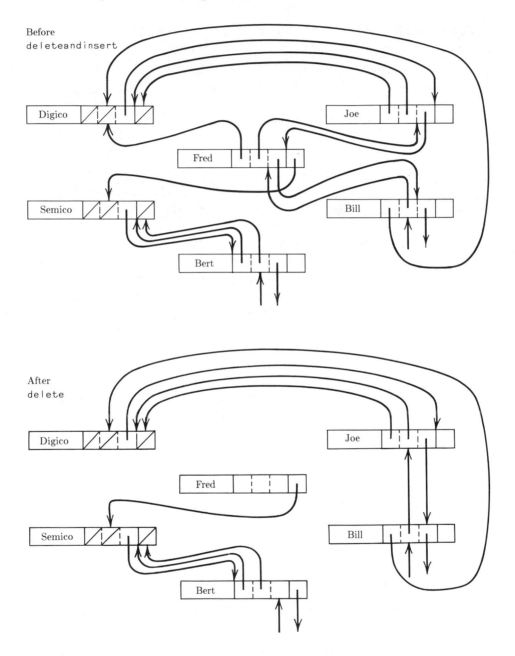

Figure 8.13 Hacker's Scalpers lists.

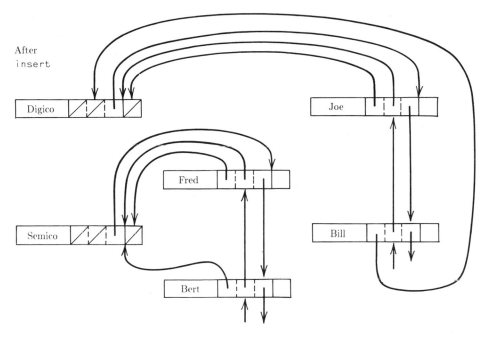

Figure 8.14 Hackers' Scalpers lists (continued).

Problems and Projects

1. Draw before-and-after diagrams that illustrate the effect of the procedure `insertafter` given in Proverb 63, when it is called for the head of a list, in the case that

    (a) The list is empty.

    (b) The list has one node.

    (c) The list has two or more nodes.

2. Computers are frequently used to eliminate duplicates from a list. Examples include lists of signatures on petitions for elections, lists of names and addresses for mailing advertising materials, lists of social

security numbers for distributing welfare payments, etc. Using the procedures outlined in Proverbs 62 through 66, write a program that creates a linked list of characters input at the terminal and that eliminates duplicates from the list, keeping only the first instance of each character.

3. For each of the statements below, draw a diagram that shows how execution of the statement affects the given diagram.

    (a) p := q

    (b) p↑.next := q↑.next

    (c) p↑ := q↑

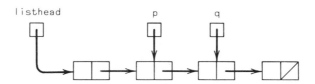

4. It is necessary, of course, to keep track of all of your special friends, and so you decide to set up a file of records containing the last name, first name, middle initial, address, telephone number, birth date, and hobbies of each of your friends. Write a program that reads these records in at the terminal, stores them in a linked list, writes them out to the screen, and then writes them to a file. The file should be a file of records, not a textfile.

    Modify the program, so that after the first time the program is run, the contents of the file are copied into the linked list and you then have the option of (a) adding a record to those already in the list, (b) deleting the record of an individual whose name is specified, and (c) changing the record of an individual whose name is specified. When you are finished, the program should copy the modified collection of records back to the file, so that the file then contains the same records as the linked list.

5. Write a complete program for the No Doubt About It Insurance Company, which uses a linked list ordered by clients' names and the insertion and deletion procedures outlined in Proverbs 63 and 65.

6. Queues are frequently encountered in banks, in supermarkets, and in computing. A common application in computer science is that of job scheduling in a time-sharing system. On arrival, a job is entered at the end of a job queue. When it reaches the front of the queue, it is removed and given a fraction of a second of processor time (a time slice). If the job does not finish in the allotted time, it is re-entered at the end of the job queue.

   Write a declaration to implement a queue as a linked list, with pointers to the front and rear of the list. Each node should contain the number of the next job to be processed by the computer and a pointer to the next node in the list, as illustrated below.

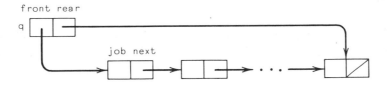

   Now write

   (a) A function to determine whether or not a queue is empty.

   (b) A procedure to insert a new node at the end of the queue.

   (c) A procedure to remove a node from the front of the queue.

   Don't forget to consider the special cases of an empty queue and a queue with just one node in it.

7. Consider, again, the appointments calendar described in Proverb 11. Write a program that uses a linked list to represent the calendar and procedures and functions to implement the calendar operations.

8. The following function is supposed to count the number of nodes in a linked list. Rewrite the function so that it works properly. If you need help, see Proverb 66.

```
function numberofnodes(listhead: listptr): nonnegint;
var
    p: listptr;
    numnodes: nonnegint;
begin
    p := listhead;
    numnodes := 0;
    while p↑.next <> nil do
        begin
            numnodes := numnodes + 1;
            p := p↑.next
        end;
    numberofnodes := numnodes
end;
```

9. Efficiency is of primary concern in the construction of symbol tables for compilers. A method that is quite efficient uses the following table format:

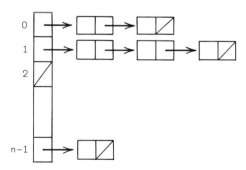

An entry in the table is a pointer that points to a linked list of records, each of which contains a word (the key) and associated data, such as whether or not the word is a reserved word and its type if it is a variable declared by the user. Several words may correspond to the same location.

Write a declaration for a table such as that described above. Then write a Pascal procedure that reads in words and associated data and builds such a table. You may assume the existence of a function called index that takes a word and returns a value in the range 0 to n-1. This represents the location in the table at which the record containing the word and its associated data will be entered. Enter the record at the beginning of the list at this location.

10. Design and write a complete Pascal program for Hacker's Scalpers that uses the linked list structure described in Proverb 67 and that enables the Scalpers to carry out their business. (And who knows, if you keep your pointers straight, you may even find your own name on their list!)

11. As the owner of the Get Outta Town Travel Service, you need an airline flight scheduling program. First, write a program to create a file of records (with 25 records or more); each of the records contains a departure city and time, an arrival city and time, the name of an airline, and a flight number.

    Next, write a program that, in its first phase, creates a list structure of airline flight information. The list structure will contain a list of nodes for departure cities. Each of these departure city nodes will contain the name of the city and a pointer to a list of arrival cities. Each of the nodes in a list of arrival cities will contain the name of the city and a pointer to a list of flights. Each of the nodes in a list of flights will contain a departure time and an arrival time. Thus, the structure will look like the following diagram:

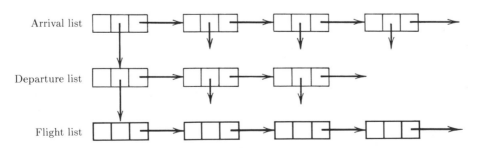

The second phase of the program will accept a customer's request for a flight from a particular departure city X to a particular arrival city Y and then, by traversing the list structure, will try to find a flight that fills this request. The program should be capable of handling any number of customers. You may assume that a flight from X to Y involves, at most, one change, that is, either it is a direct flight or it involves just one change at a third city Z. Also assume that the layover, or turnaround time, at Z is at least 30 minutes and that the next connecting flight is always chosen.

The program will print out all flights from X to Y. If the program finds a direct flight, it will print out the departure city and time, the airline and flight number, and the arrival city and time. If a third city Z is involved, it will also print out the name of this city along with the arrival and departure times and the connecting airline and flight number. If no flight is available between the requested departure and arrival points, it will print out a message to that effect.

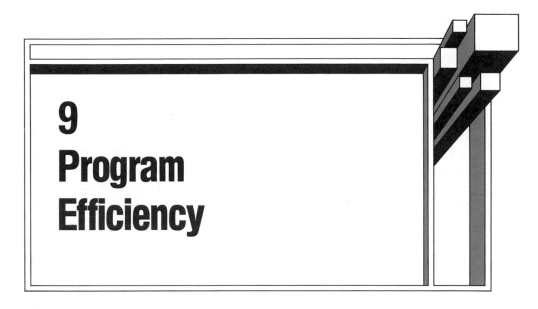

9
Program
Efficiency

The time to think about efficiency is before you start writing your program. If you wait until your program runs too slowly, or uses more memory than is available, most of the factors that affect efficiency are already determined, and only minor improvements are possible without major surgery.

While you are designing your data structures, consider the amount of space they will occupy. While you are designing your algorithms, consider the time it will take to execute them. Then concentrate your efforts on the data structures and the algorithms that will result in the greatest improvements. Your skill as a programmer will be reflected in the efficiency of your programs.

68 Efficiency deficiency?
Find a better algorithm.

The most important consideration in developing efficient computer programs is the overall design of the program and the choice of efficient data structures and algorithms. Often, several different algorithms or implementations are available to solve the same problem. The amount of time and space required by a program depend on exactly how the algorithm is implemented to create the program. But the differences between algorithms are often much more important then the effects of careful implementation.

The improvement resulting from a very skillful implementation may cause the program to run two or three times faster, a useful improvement. A different algorithm, even inefficiently implemented, might run hundreds or thousands of times faster. For example, the simplest and most obvious sorting algorithm, Bubblesort, typically needs about 1,000,000 operations to sort an array of 1000 items. (We used the Bubblesort algorithm in the example in Proverb 26.)

A less obvious, but still quite simple, algorithm, Quicksort, can sort the same array in typically 10,000 operations. The Quicksort algorithm is given below. Quicksort is so much more efficient an algorithm than Bubblesort that if you have any quantity of data (say over 20 items), it is really not worth considering Bubblesort at all.

```
(* This procedure sorts the elements of an array *)
(* into increasing order.  It rearranges the      *)
(* elements and splits the array into two         *)
(* subsections so that all the elements in the    *)
(* first section are less than all the elements   *)
(* in the second section.  It then sorts each     *)
(* section recursively.                           *)

procedure quicksort(var a: arraytype;
                    low, high: index);
var
   i: index;

   procedure split(var a: arraytype; low, high: index;
                   var i: index);
   var
      x: integer;
      up, down: index;
   begin (* Split *)
      i := low;
      x := a[i];
      up := low;
      down := high;
```

```
    while up < down do
      begin
        while (down > up) and (a[down] > x) do
          down := down - 1;
        if down > up then
          begin
            a[i] := a[down];
            i := down
          end;
        while (up < down) and (a[up] <= x) do
          up := up + 1;
        if up < down then
          begin
            a[i] := a[up];
            i := up
          end
      end;
    a[i] := x
  end; (* Split *)
begin (* Quicksort *)
  if low < high then
    begin
      split(a, low, high, i);
      if i > low + 1 then
        quicksort(a, low, i-1);
      if i < high - 1 then
        quicksort(a, i+1, high)
    end
end; (* Quicksort *)
```

You may choose to implement the Quicksort algorithm iteratively, rather than recursively, to obtain even greater efficiency. But the main increase in efficiency will have been obtained from the Quicksort algorithm itself, even in its recursive form. In trying to write the most efficient code, you should therefore spend most of your time making sure that you have used efficient algorithms.

It is often necessary to consider the program as a whole and, thus, the context in which each part of the program will be used, rather than to consider each part individually. For example, it may be desirable to incur a heavy expense at one point in the program, so as to speed up other parts of the program. Suppose, in particular, that you are searching for the largest element in an array and removing it, repeatedly. It may be preferable for you to incur the cost of sorting the array when you create it. In order to decide, you will need to compare the time it takes to sort the array initially with the time it takes to search the array repeatedly for the largest element.

Determining the best algorithm for a particular task can be a complicated process, often involving sophisticated mathematical analysis. A great deal of research has been done in developing efficient algorithms for commonly performed computing tasks, such as sorting and searching.[1] You're well advised to take an analysis of algorithms course in which the time and space efficiency of algorithms is studied in detail. Analyzing the efficiency of algorithms can be difficult, but it's a skill you should develop to enable you to choose between alternative algorithms and concentrate your programming efforts on where they'll do the most good.

69 Put a price on your time.

As the cost of machine time and memory decreases and the cost of your time as a programmer increases, you must decide whether it's worth your time to make efficiency changes in your programs. If a program is to be used only once, then the additional time that you spend in making your program more efficient and getting it to run may not be worth the savings in computer time or memory. But if the program is to be used many times (e.g., if the program is an editor or compiler), then increasing the efficiency may be worthwhile.

For most algorithms, the number of data items being processed affects the running time most significantly. This might be the number

---

[1]See, for example, Donald E. Knuth, *Sorting and Searching, The Art of Computer Programming*, Vol. 3 (Addison-Wesley, Reading, Massachusetts, 1973).

of components in an array being sorted, the number of records in a file being searched, or the number of nodes in a linked list being traversed. If a program is to be used for a large number of data items, then it may be worthwhile to try to increase the efficiency by finding a better algorithm.

An algorithm's performance in terms of its time (or space) requirements is usually characterized as a function, T (or S), of the number n of data items. This function is often quite complicated and is therefore usually approximated by a much simpler function, F. More precisely, we say that "T is of the order of F," or "T is big O of F," and we write $T(n) = O(F(n))$, if there exist constants c and N, such that

$$|T(n)| \leq c|F(n)| \text{ for all } n \geq N.$$

For example, if $T(n) = 2n^2 - 6n + 30$, then $T(n) = O(F(n))$, where $F(n) = n^2$, because there exist constants $c = 2$ and $N = 5$, such that

$$|T(n)| = \left|2n^2 - 6n + 30\right| \leq 2\left|n^2\right| = c|F(n)| \text{ for all } n \geq N = 5.$$

Likewise, if $T(n) = 7n^3 + 3n^2 + 8$, then $T(n) = O(F(n))$, where $F(n) = n^3$, because there exist constants $c = 10$ and $N = 2$, such that

$$|T(n)| = \left|7n^3 + 3n^2 + 8\right| \leq 10\left|n^3\right| = c|F(n)| \text{ for all } n \geq N = 2.$$

The order terminology expresses the fact that we're interested in approximating the performance of an algorithm by the dominant term of a function, ignoring the smaller terms and constants. It gives us a rough idea of the inherent difficulty or complexity of an algorithm, independent of the particular computer that might be used to implement it.

The complexity of an algorithm is usually described in terms of one of a few standard functions:

$$1, \log_2 n, n, n\log_2 n, n^2, n^3, \dots, 2^n$$

An algorithm is said to be polynomial if its running time is $T = O(n^k)$. In particular, it is constant if $k = 0$, linear if $k = 1$, quadratic if $k = 2$, cubic if $k = 3$, etc. An algorithm is called logarithmic if its running time is $T = O(\log_2 n)$, and it is exponential if its running time is $T = O(2^n)$. These functions tell us how the cost of solving a problem increases as n increases. For example, if $T = O(n^2)$ and the size of the input n is doubled, then the running time is increased fourfold, because $(2n)^2 = 4n^2$. If $T = O(n^3)$ and n is doubled, then the running time is increased eightfold, because $(2n)^3 = 8n^2$, etc. However, if $T = O(2^n)$ and n is doubled, then the running time is squared (bad news!), because $2^{2n} = (2^n)^2$.

When using the order notation to decide whether to use one algorithm rather than another, you must be careful to consider not only the function F but also the constant c of proportionality and the number n of data items. For small values of n an algorithm of higher order may perform better than an algorithm of lower order, because the algorithm of higher order may have a smaller constant of proportionality than the algorithm of lower order.

But for large values of n, the algorithm of lower order will usually be far superior. If, for example, our machine performs one instruction per microsecond (i.e., 10^6 instructions per second), if the number of data items is $n = 10^2$, and if it takes $1\,\mu\text{sec}$ (microsecond) to process each data item, then a logarithmic algorithm would require only about

$$\log_2 n = \log_2 10^2 \sim 7\,\mu\text{sec},$$

whereas an exponential algorithm would take

$$2^n = 2^{10^2} \sim 10^{30}\,\mu\text{sec} \sim 2.7 \times 10^{16}\ \text{years!}$$

The following table shows more of these figures.

	1	$\log_2 n$	n	$n \log_2 n$	n^2	n^3	2^n
10	1	3.322	10	33.22	10^2	10^3	$2^{10} \sim 10^3$
10^2	1	6.644	10^2	664.4	10^4	10^6	$2^{10^2} \sim 10^{30}$
10^3	1	9.966	10^3	9966.0	10^6	10^9	$2^{10^3} \sim 10^{301}$
10^4	1	13.287	10^4	132,877	10^8	10^{12}	$2^{10^4} \sim 10^{3010}$

Let's now consider a few simple examples that illustrate the notion of order. In analyzing an algorithm, we often count the number of times a particular arithmetic operation is performed or the number of comparisons that are made, etc. For example, consider the standard algorithm for matrix multiplication.

```
for i := 1 to n do
   for j := 1 to n do
      begin
         c[i,j] := 0;
         for k := 1 to n do
            c[i,j] := c[i,j] + a[i,k]*b[k,j]
      end;
```

This algorithm is of order n^3, because the operations of addition and multiplication are each done once in the innermost loop, the nesting of loops is three deep, and each of the loops is executed n times.

In analyzing an algorithm, usually the average and worst case behaviors of the algorithm are considered. The average behavior gives the amount of time that a program might be expected to take when given typical input data. The worst case gives the amount of time that a program would take, given the worst possible data.

For example, consider linear search of an ordered list. In the worst case, the item we're searching for is the last item, and we must examine all n values. In the average case, assuming that all positions are equally likely, the probability that the item we're searching for occurs in a particular position is $1/n$, and the average number of comparisons is

$$\frac{1}{n} \times 1 + \frac{1}{n} \times 2 + \ldots + \frac{1}{n} \times n = \frac{1}{n} \times (1 + 2 + \ldots + n) = \frac{1}{n} \times \frac{n(n+1)}{2} = \frac{n+1}{2}$$

Thus, in both the average and worst cases, this algorithm is of order n.

Characterizing the efficiency of an algorithm in terms of its average and worst case behaviors can be somewhat misleading, however. The average behavior of an algorithm may not be at all representative of the data actually used. Furthermore, although an algorithm is $O(2^n)$ in the worst case, it might be quite satisfactory in practice, because the worst case may never be encountered. You really must consider the actual data being used to get an accurate assessment of the efficiency of an algorithm.

70 A need for speed? Take time to time.

90% of the time is spend in 10% of the code.

Before making efficiency changes, find this 10% and put your efforts into improving the efficiency there. Beware of preconceptions about where time is being spent. Avoid looking in the wrong place for improvements. Take measurements before making efficiency changes!

To measure the efficiency of your program, include counters in your program so that you can determine which statements are executed most often. Set up an array count, initialize the index i, and include the statement

```
count[i] := count[i] + 1;
```

immediately after the ith statement so that you can see how many times it is executed. For example, in a sorting routine you might count the number of comparisons or the number of exchanges made within a loop.

You might also time the execution of procedures, functions, and program fragments. Most systems include a run-time clock function that you can use to determine how much time is spent executing a particular piece of code. Set up an array, time, initialize the indices i and j, and include the statements

```
time[i,j] := clock;
(* Before the ith call to procedure j. *)
        .
        .
(* After the ith call to procedure j. *)
elapsedtime[i,j] := clock - time[i,j];
```

in your program around the call to the jth procedure. The value of elapsedtime[i,j] then gives you the amount of time it took for the ith execution of procedure j.

A complete listing of counts and timings for a particular run of a program is referred to as an execution profile. Many computer centers provide canned programs, often referred to as profilers, which provide an execution profile of a program. Although specific implementations of profilers differ from installation to installation, profilers can be used to

- Count the number of times a specific procedure or function is called.

- Compute the percentage of execution time spent in each procedure or function.

- List the program code, complete with information on the number of times each line or group of lines (loop, if-then-else block, sequence of lines, etc.) is executed.

Profilers can be used to locate loops that are executed an excessive amount of time; in particular, they can be used to identify infinite loops. They can also be used to locate lines that have not been executed and to identify logic errors that prevent the lines from being executed. Profilers are most valuable for drawing attention to the portions of a program that dominate execution time. Such information can be used for optimization of your code.

Consult your professor or computer lab consultant for information about the execution profilers that may be available at your local computer center. Most profilers have only a few commands, so it probably won't take much time to learn to use one. Request a hard copy of the documentation that describes the execution profiler available for the particular system you are using.

71 Waste in loops is waste indeed.

Generally, most of the time used by a program is spent in executing a few instructions nested deep within the loop structure of a program. To increase the efficiency of your program, concentrate on increasing the efficiency of the inner loops. Make sure that you do not put unnecessary expensive instructions in a loop that must be executed many times. Here are a few suggestions for improving the efficiency of loops.

1. Remove constant operations from inside loops, using the basic properties of integers and real numbers. For example, instead of writing

```
sum := 0;
for i := 1 to 1000 do
    sum := sum + c * x[i];
```

use the distributive property and write

```
sum := 0;
for i := 1 to 1000 do
    sum := sum + x[i];
sum := c * sum;
```

In the first version, the multiplication is done 1000 times; in the second version, it is done only once.

2. Reduce the number of references to arrays inside loops. Consider the following example in which we find the maximum element of an array and its position in the array.

```
(* This fragment finds the maximum *)
(* element of an array and its      *)
(* position in the array.           *)

k := 1;
for i := 2 to n do
    if a[i] > a[k] then
        k := i;
max := a[k];
```

In the comparison within the loop, we have two array references a[i] and a[k], whereas we could get by with just one, as follows:

```
(* This fragment finds the maximum *)
(* element of an array and its      *)
(* position in the array.           *)

k := 1;
max := a[1];
for i := 2 to n do
   if a[i] > max then
      begin
         max := a[i];
         k := i
      end;
```

3. Iterate a loop only as many times as is necessary to solve the problem at hand. For example, if a linear search is used to search for a particular name in an alphabetically ordered list, the search should be terminated at the point where it is known that the name could not occur later. In place of writing

```
while not eof(namefile) and
      (namesought <> currentname) do
   get(namefile);
```

write

```
while not eof(namefile) and
      (namesought < currentname) do
   get(namefile);
```

"Hotshot" programmers sometimes try to speed up an algorithm by trying to implement it, using the least number of loops. Although this is often possible, it usually makes programs much harder to read and debug. When a more efficient solution to a problem is required, it is far better to try to improve the algorithm than to employ programming tricks that obscure what is being done.

72 Spaced out runs out of space.

A program requires storage space for instructions, constants, variables, and input data, and also for manipulating data and storing information needed to carry out its computation. The problem of limited storage space is more serious on small personal computers than on large mainframes. If you get a message like

> Ran out of memory

or

> Workspace is full

you may be able to extend the amount of space allocated to your program by issuing some special command. Ask one of your lab assistants or fellow programmers about this, or refer to the manual. If it's not possible to increase the amount of work space, you will have to find some means of economizing on the amount of space used by your program.

In trying to economize on storage space, remember that some data structures require more space than others to store the same data. For example, we might have the following declaration:

```
type
  mnftype = (chrysler,ford,generalmotors);
  astring = array[1..30] of char;
  colors = (black,blue,green,red,white,yellow);
  wrntyrecord = ...;
  carrecord = record
                manufacturer: mnftype;
                make, model: astring;
                color: colors;
                identificationnumber: integer;
                price: real;
                warranty: wrntyrecord
              end;
  cararray = array[1..1000] of carrecord;
var
  cars: cararray;
```

If, however, an automobile manufacturer gives the same warranty for each of its cars, then we do not really need to keep 1000 copies of this warranty information, but only one copy for each manufacturer. The warranty information for the various manufacturers should be kept separately, rather than in each of these 1000 records. The following declaration is, therefore, preferable:

```
type
    mnftype = (chrysler,ford,generalmotors);
    astring = array[1..30] of char;
    colors = (black,blue,green,red,white,yellow);
    wrntyrecord = ...;
    wrntyarray = array[mnftype] of wrntyrecord;
    carrecord = record
                    manufacturer: mnftype;
                    make, model: astring;
                    color: colors;
                    identificationnumber: integer;
                    price: real
                end;
    cararray = array[1..1000] of carrecord;
var
    warranty: wrntyarray;
    cars: cararray;
```

Then, when we need the warranty information for a particular car, we check the manufacturer and look up the warranty for that manufacturer. Thus, to access the warranty for the ith car, we would write `warranty[cars[i].manufacturer]`.

Duplicated information is not merely a waste of space but can lead to logical problems. For example, if we have only a single copy of the warranty, we do not need to worry about making certain that all of the copies are consistent. Moreover, we should design our structures so that we do not "lose" the warranty as soon as we sell the car and remove it from the stock list. If you take a database course, you will learn techniques for avoiding such problems.

Another structure that can save space is the variant record. Instead of declaring a record, some of whose fields are not used all of the time, we can use a variant record. For example, in writing a program to create a bibliography, we might include the following record declaration:

```
type
    astring = array[1..30] of char;
    biblioentry = record
                    title,author: astring;
                    date: 1900..1985;
                    publisher, city: astring;
                    journal: astring;
                    volume, number: 1..100;
                    firstpage, lastpage: 1..1000
                  end;
    bibliography = array[1..10000] of biblioentry;
```

However, if the bibliography entry is a book, then some of the fields are not relevant, namely the journal, volume, number, firstpage, and lastpage fields; whereas if the entry is an article, then the publisher and city fields are not relevant. To make the best use of the space allocated for the record, we should declare a variant record, as follows:

```
type
    astring = array[1..30] of char;
    sourcetype = (book, magazine);
    biblioentry = record
                    title, author: astring;
                    date: 1900..1985;
                    case sourcetag: sourcetype of
                        book: (publisher, city: astring);
                        article: (journal: astring;
                                  volume, number: 1..100;
                                  firstpage,lastpage:1..1000)
                  end;
    bibliography = array[1..10000] of biblioentry;
```

This variant record is illustrated in Fig. 9.1.

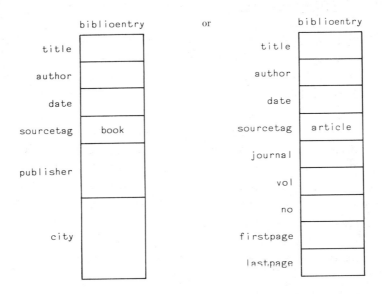

Figure 9.1 Variant record.

The linked list is another data structure that can be a space saver. For example, we can use either an array or a linked list to store the coefficients of a polynomial. If the polynomial is of high degree, but has lots of coefficients that are 0, then a linked list is a more efficient implementation because only the nonzero coefficients need be stored. For example, the polynomial $p(x) = x^{1000} - x^{500} + 25$ requires an array with 1001 components to store all of its coefficients, but because only three coefficients are nonzero, it can be represented by using a linked list with just three components (Fig. 9.2).

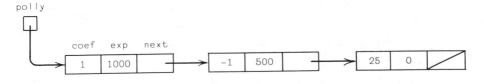

Figure 9.2 Linked list representation of a polynomial.

73 All is relative in space and time.

Needless to say, it is desirable to design algorithms that are economical in their use of both processor space and time, but usually there is a time/space tradeoff. One algorithm may use more space, whereas the other uses more time. Often, the equipment available will dictate whether you need to economize on space or time.

For example, we can arrange our data in a table so that the table is indexed directly by the key values of the data. Thus, in Fig. 9.3 we have placed the data for part number 0003 in the third location of the table. Access in a table such as this is very fast because only a single location need be accessed, regardless of the table size. However, such a table requires one entry for every possible value of the key. If only a few of the key values actually occur, this will be a very inefficient use of space. We have gained a time advantage at the cost of extra space.

partnumber	description
0003	Nut
0005	Bolt
0009	Screw
0012	Nail
0014	Washer

Figure 9.3 Table indexed by key values.

At the other extreme, we might arrange our data in a linked list (Fig. 9.4). Each entry needs some additional space for the pointers that link the entries together into a list, but the data need exactly as many entries as there are data items to store. However, this economy in space is bought at the price of the time it takes to search the list to find the data. The search must begin with the first entry in the list and must examine each entry in turn, until the needed item is found. On average, about half of the entries in the list must be accessed during each search. For example, for a list of 1000 items, 500 must be accessed during a search.

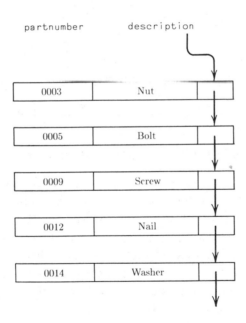

partnumber   description

0003	Nut
0005	Bolt
0009	Screw
0012	Nail
0014	Washer

Figure 9.4 Linked list.

A different approach can greatly speed up the search. By arranging our data in order in an array (see Fig. 9.5), we can use the binary search technique described in Proverb 56. The advantage of the binary search is that the cost for an n element array is of order $\log_2 n$. With it, we can search a 1000-entry array in, at most, 10 steps, a big improvement on the linked list search. The price is that we must provide an array large enough to contain the data. If we know exactly how much data we will have to process, this can be quite efficient. But, often, we do not know that, and to accommodate the worst case we must provide an array that is much bigger than is necessary for most of the data.

partnumber	description
0003	Nut
0005	Bolt
0009	Screw
0012	Nail
0014	Washer
0019	Rivit
0023	Wire
0024	Hinge
0028	Lock

Figure 9.5 Table with key values in increasing order.

Yet another approach is to use hashing techniques, which are quite efficient in their use of both time and space. The particular hashing techniques used depend, to a great extent, on the nature of the data and on the computer equipment that is available. Hashing techniques are used in the design of computer systems where efficiency is a very important consideration. Such techniques are really beyond the scope of this book, but if you take a course in data structures, you will probably study hashing techniques in detail.

The decision that you make, however, may be not how to organize the data for storage, but whether to store the data at all. Sometimes, you will have to decide between the following alternatives:

- The data may be computed once and stored for subsequent reference. This is computationally efficient but may require too much storage space. You then have to consider storing the data in a disk file instead of in the main memory of the computer.

- The data, or more probably part of the data, may be recomputed each time that they are needed. This is computationally expensive but may be the only feasible approach if the potential data size is large.

For example, consider Flying Flo, the distributor for the Florida Flowering Flyswatter, who had to solve the traveling saleswoman problem to decide the order in which to visit various cities so as to minimize the total distance that she traveled (see Chapter 7, Problem 8). To solve her problem, we assumed the existence of a function distance to provide the distance between any two cities.

We could implement this function (as we did in Problem 8) using a square array indexed by the two cities, making retrieval of the desired information very simple. But, if there are 10,000 cities potentially requiring fly extermination, then the size of the array (100,000,000 entries!) will be a problem.

As an alternative, we can compute the distance between two cities on demand, starting with information only about distances between neighboring cities. Here, to keep our example simple, we assume that there are, at most, four neighboring cities (as in Fig. 9.6), and we store the information about them in the array road. Each element of this array contains two fields, one for the destination of the road and the other for the distance.

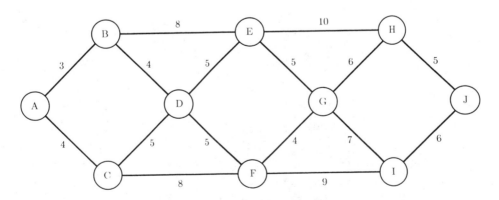

Figure 9.6 Typical data for the breadth-first search algorithm.

The distance function given below is based on a very useful algorithm, the breadth-first search algorithm. At each stage, we have a set of cities that are done; for each of these cities, we know its distance from the starting city. We also have a set of cities that are unseen and a third set of cities that are pending. The object of the program is to include cities, one at a time, in the done set.

Every time a city is included in the done set, we consider each of its four neighbors to see if we can improve its distance from the starting city; if we can, we include it in the pending set. We search the pending set to find the city closest to the starting city. We make that city the next one to be moved to the done set, because consideration of other cities in the pending set cannot improve the distance for they are even farther away.

```
const
   maxcity = 10;
   maxadjacent = 4;
type
   citytype = 1..maxcity;
   adjacenttype = 1..maxadjacent;
   miles = 0..10000;
   rectype = record
                dist: miles;
                dest: citytype
             end;
   roadtype = array[citytype,adjacenttype] of rectype;
var
   road: roadtype;
function distance(citya, cityb: citytype): miles;
type
   status = (done, pending, unseen);
var
   citystatus: array[citytype] of status;
   citydistance: array[citytype] of miles;
   i, nextcity: citytype;
   k: adjacenttype;
   nextdistance: miles;
```

```
begin (* Distance *)
  for i := 1 to maxcity do
    begin
      citystatus[i] := unseen;
      citydistance[i] := 9999
    end;
  citystatus[citya] := done;
  citydistance[citya] := 0;
  nextcity := citya;
  nextdistance := 0;
  while (citystatus[cityb] <> done) and
        (nextdistance < 9999) do
    begin
      for k := 1 to maxadjacent do
        begin
          if nextdistance + road[nextcity,k].dist <
             citydistance[road[nextcity,k].dest] then
            begin
              citystatus[road[nextcity,k].dest] :=
                pending;
              citydistance[road[nextcity,k].dest] :=
                nextdistance + road[nextcity,k].dist
            end
        end;
      nextdistance := 9999;
      for i := 1 to maxcity do
        if (citystatus[i] = pending) and
           (citydistance[i] < nextdistance) then
          begin
            nextdistance := citydistance[i];
            nextcity := i
          end;
      citystatus[nextcity] := done
    end;
  distance := citydistance[cityb]
end; (* Distance *)
```

You will learn more about breadth-first search in subsequent computer courses, about when to use it, and about how to code it more efficiently. Study it well, and you will find that there are fewer "flies" on your program.

74 Make it clear what you are making fast.

Concern for writing very fast, tight code should come last, not first. Your first concern should be writing clear, correct programs. Don't sacrifice clarity for small gains in efficiency.

However, when you need to increase coding efficiency, the first place to try to economize (as we have already pointed out in Proverb 71) is in the most frequently executed portions of your program, for example, the innermost loop in a nest of loops or the branch of an if-then-else statement that is executed most often. Leave the rest of the program alone. The efficiency of seldom run code does not matter, but the correctness and clarity of it does.

Here are a few more hints that will help you to increase coding efficiency and reduce program run time.

- Avoid using the type real when the type integer should be used instead. Calculation with real numbers is more complex and may be much more expensive. On a small computer the cost of using real numbers rather than integers may be as much as 100 times as great.

- Prefer + and − to × and /. Prefer × to / and exponentiation. The relative speed of these operations depends on your particular computer. Exponentiation is typically 50 to 100 times slower than multiplication.

- Avoid computing the same expression more than once. Instead, compute the expression, assign it to a variable, and use the variable in place of the expression.

- Use nested **if** statements rather than **and** and **or**. The truth or falsity of a boolean expression may be determined by its first subexpression, in which case you won't have to evaluate its other subexpressions.

- Simplify the boolean expressions that control loops. Remember, such a boolean expression must be evaluated each time the loop is executed.

- Keep array subscripts inside loops as simple as possible. Some compilers can generate more efficient code for simple subscripts.

- Avoid functions with side effects. These are difficult for the code optimizer of your compiler.

- Take the code of a procedure or function and place it in line at the point from which it is called. But do not do this too much—it can use up a lot of space.

Above all, remember that modifications made in a program, once it has been written, will not usually have much effect on the efficiency of a program. The real gains in efficiency are in the algorithm you choose and not in the code.

Problems and Projects

1. Show that $T(n) = O(F(n))$ by finding constants c and N, such that $|T(n)| \leq |F(n)|$ for all $n \geq N$.

    (a) $T(n) = 7n^2 - 3n + 5$, $F(n) = n^2$.

    (b) $T(n) = 2n^3 + 4n^2 + 8n + 16$, $F(n) = n^3$.

    (c) $T(n) = n + \log_2 n$, $F(n) = n$.

2. In an article called "Algorithms," which appeared in the April 1977 issue of *Scientific American*, Donald Knuth discusses various searching algorithms and their efficiency. Get a copy of this article and read it. Write a one-page summary of what you have learned from this article.

3. Consider the following algorithm for matrix multiplication:

```
for i := 1 to n do
  for j := 1 to n do
    c[i,j] := 0;
  for k := 1 to n do
    for i := 1 to n do
      for j := 1 to n do
        c[i,j] := c[i,j] + a[i,k]*b[k,j];
```

What is the order of this algorithm? See Proverb 69 for a discussion of the concept of order.

4. Design an algorithm to reverse the elements of a one-dimensional integer array whose length is n. Then give the time and space complexities of your algorithm in terms of the "big O" notation (read Proverb 69 again, if necessary).

5. Proverb 70 describes the use of timing statements to profile a program. Choose a program that has several procedures and functions (if you wrote the payroll program in Chapter 4, Problem 6, this would be a good choice). Profile the program, using your own timing statements. Identify the procedures and functions that should be optimized and those that are not worth the bother.

6. To evaluate a polynomial $a_n x^n + a_{n-1} x^{n-1} + ... + a_1 x + a_0$, we can use the standard algorithm

$$a_n \underbrace{xx...x}_{n} + a_{n-1} \underbrace{xx...x}_{n-1} + ... + a_1 x + a_0$$

Alternatively, we can use a method called Horner's method, in which the polynomial is written as follows:

$$(((a_n x + a_{n-1})x + a_{n-2})x + ... + a_1)x + a_0$$

How many additions and multiplications are required to evaluate a polynomial, using (a) the standard algorithm and (b) Horner's method? Express your answer in terms of the degree n of the polynomial.

Write a Pascal program that includes functions for each of these algorithms, and determine how much time is used by each to evaluate
a polynomial of degree (a) 4, (b) 16, and (c) 32. How do these two
methods compare for accuracy?

7. Consult one of your computer lab assistants or more experienced
colleagues about the execution profilers that may be available at
your local computer center. If your computer center has one, use it
to create a profile of one of the programs that you have written
from this text.

8. After writing the banking program in Chapter 6, Problem 11, determine what percentage of its execution time is spent

(a) Reading and validating input.

(b) Processing.

(c) Output.

10
Testing
and Debugging

All programmers have experienced the trials and tribulations of testing and debugging their programs. The testing and debugging phase of program development includes testing the program for the existence of errors, locating the errors by looking at the values of the program variables, correcting the errors, and testing the program again to see that those errors have been eliminated.

Without thoughtful preparation, the testing and debugging phase can literally lead to nightmares! However, the proverbs in this chapter are designed to lessen the pain of these tasks and, perhaps, make portions of this phase of program development even pleasurable for you. In any event, we're confident that by applying these proverbs, you can save yourself a lot of time and trouble.

75 Testing if it's right
will only prove it wrong.

Initially, you may think that this proverb says that testing is rather fruitless, but that's not what is intended. Instead, the point is that running a few tests on your program cannot **prove** that there is **nothing** wrong with your code, but it can reveal the existence of errors. Moreover, testing does not tell you what is wrong or where the error occurs, but only that something is wrong with your program.

To test your program, you will need to select specific input values and run the program to see if it produces the correct answers for those particular values. Because only a limited set of input values are ever used (after all, you're not going to spend the rest of your life testing the code), testing cannot prove that your program is correct, but it can reveal a problem when your program produces a wrong answer.

Once you have determined the existence of a problem, either on the basis of the results produced by testing or, perhaps, on the basis of a problem reported by a user, you can then diagnose the problem. To determine what the error is and to locate the precise point in your program where the error occurs, you will need to look at the values of the variables in your program at run time. You can do this by making use of the debugging aids of your Pascal system or by inserting debugging write statements in your program to trace the values of the variables (more on this in Proverb 79).

Frequently, additional testing will be required to isolate the problem more specifically; you may need to trace the values of additional variables in order to detect what is wrong, and you may need to try additional test cases, particularly to reduce a complex condition into a simple test case that still provokes the error but is easier to understand. Once you have located the error, you can then go ahead and make the corrections in your code and also the corresponding corrections in your documentation. (We'll talk about documentation and its maintenance in the final chapter of this book.) You should then test the program again to see that the error has, indeed, been eliminated.

Unfortunately, the method of testing is often flawed, not only because the tests may be inadequate but also because programmers may fail to look at the results carefully enough to notice the errors. Nonetheless, it's worth your time to learn the truth about the quality of your code during the testing phase, because if you don't find the errors in your program, somebody else probably will (whether it be your instructor, your boss, or some guy who spent several hundred dollars for your program). If you have been thorough in your testing, you will receive no news about the errors in your programs, and that **is** good news!

76 Remember the fundamental principle of debugging.

The fundamental principle of debugging states

> The single, most useful debugging aid is a
> well-written, well-organized, well-structured program.

Debugging is the search-and-rescue portion of a programmer's job. Most programmers become concerned about debugging code early on in their careers (often, just after running their first program). For programmers who have not written well-organized, well-structured programs, debugging can be a tedious, mind-boggling, and traumatic experience. But even then, it helps to prepare for debugging sessions during the design and development phase by using stubs (see Proverb 77) and by including debugging write statements in your programs (see Proverb 79).

You should expect your program to contain bugs, and your objective in the testing and debugging phase must be to find bugs. Do not try to show that there are none. By making it your objective to find bugs and getting pleasure out of finding them, debugging can be fun, and you will do a better job of it. If you start by believing that your program is entirely correct, you are sure to be disappointed and frustrated, and you will not do as good a job of debugging.

Always have a rational plan for finding the bugs in a program. If you are sitting at a terminal and you find that you have a bug in your program, get a listing of the program and a set of sample tests. Use the program listing and its results, textbooks and reference manuals, debugging aids, and your own experience to identify the cause of your problem before you make any changes. In the unlikely event that you cannot isolate the problem and are unsure of how to proceed, seek competent professional help. Be wary of worthless advice.

Above all, remember the fundamental principle of debugging. By writing well-organized, well-structured programs, you will reduce the number of bugs in your programs and will make it easier to find the bugs that remain.

77 Test before you write the rest.

In a top-down approach to program development, the most abstract pieces of a program are built first. It's hard to test these abstract pieces until the whole program has been written, because the most abstract pieces use other pieces that haven't yet been written. The way around this is to use stubs.

A stub is a preliminary, simplified version of a procedure or function included in a program to allow compilation and execution to proceed meaningfully and to allow a program to complete without incurring errors. Stubs are used in the early stages of program development to test that a program, at its current level of development, is working properly. As soon as the details of a procedure or function are written, the procedure or function is tested, using stubs for the other procedures and functions that haven't yet been written.

A stub does not perform the task eventually intended for the procedure or function, and it lacks most of the final details. However, it must have exactly the same parameters as the eventual procedure or function. In a stub you might simply write out a message that you've reached the procedure or function. You might also write out the values of its "in" parameters. The stub should return values for its "out" parameters that enable the calling program to run to completion. The values that the procedure or function is meant to generate and that are returned to the calling program might be assigned or, alternatively, they might be read in interactively (though this can become somewhat tedious). Because the construction of a stub is so highly designed around in parameters, out parameters, and assignments to globals, a stub is quite a good specification of what the full procedure or function is trying to do.

In the following example, we give the stub structure for a program that analyzes the scores of students on a particular exam or assignment. Notice that we have set up parameters for each of the procedures and functions. Notice also that in each procedure and function we write out a message that we've reached that procedure or function. We also assign values to the out parameters of each procedure and to the name of each function.

```pascal
program assignlettergrades(input, output);
type
   index = 0..35;
   nonnegint = 0..100;
   letters = (a, b, c, d, f);
   astring = array[1..11] of char;
   arecord = record
                 idnumber: astring;
                 score: nonnegint;
                 grade: letters
              end;
   aarray = array[1..35] of arecord;
var
   numstudents, i: index;
   lowest, highest, mean: nonnegint;
   stddev: real;
   students: aarray;
procedure readdata(var a: aarray; var n: index);
begin
   writeln('In procedure readdata');
   n := 0
end;
procedure writedata(var a: aarray; n: index;
                       l, h, m: nonnegint; s: real);
begin
   writeln('In procedure writedata')
end;
function lowestscore(var a: aarray; n: index): nonnegint;
begin
   writeln('In function lowestscore');
   lowestscore := 0
end;
function highestscore(var a: aarray; n: index): nonnegint;
begin
   writeln('In function highestscore');
   highestscore := 100
end;
```

```
function meanscore(var a: aarray; n: index): nonnegint;
begin
  writeln('In function mean');
  meanscore := 50
end;
function standarddeviation(var a: aarray; n: index;
                              m: nonnegint): real;
var
  s: real;
begin
  writeln('In function standarddeviation');
  writeln('Enter the standard deviation');
  readln(s);
  standarddeviation := s
end;
procedure assigngrade(var r: arecord; s: real);
begin
  writeln('In procedure lettergrade');
  r.grade := a
end;

begin (* Main program *)
  readdata(students, numstudents);
  lowest := lowestscore(students, numstudents);
  highest := highestscore(students, numstudents);
  mean := meanscore(students, numstudents);
  stddev := standarddeviation(students,numstudents,mean);
  for i := 1 to numstudents do
    assigngrade(students[i], stddev);
  writedata(students, numstudents,
            lowest, highest, mean, stddev)
end. (* Main program *)
```

Here, the highest level procedure writedata uses the results of assigngrade, standarddeviation, mean, highest, lowest, and readdata. The next highest level procedure assigngrade uses the results of standarddeviation and readdata. The function standard-deviation, in turn, uses the results of mean and readdata, etc.

As testing proceeds, we replace each stub (starting at the highest level) with the actual code necessary to carry out its intended computation. In the example above, we would first write the code for the procedure writedata and, then, go on to write the code for the procedure assigngrade, and so on. In Problem 11 at the end of this chapter, you are asked to complete this example by writing the details of these procedures and functions, testing each one as you complete it, using stubs for the remaining procedures and functions.

78 High grade tests require choice data.

The data you select for testing your program should include

- Normal "easy" values that make finding the first bugs quicker.

- Some values for which it is easy to compute the correct results by hand.

- Values to force true and false on every condition.

- Boundary cases at the extremes of the range of data values.

- Cases in which nothing is to be done.

- Illegal cases.

It's very hard, but especially important, to test the illegal cases to make sure that your program does not produce inappropriate results or inappropriate error messages. It takes much more skill to test these cases than it does to test the easy standard ones.

Consider the following fragment:

```
while i <= samplesize do
   if (age < 18) or (age > 65) then
```

This fragment should be tested with the following extreme values: age = 17, age = 18, age = 65, age = 66, i = samplesize, and i = samplesize + 1.

Consider another example. The marketing division of Micros, Inc., a chain of computer stores, has conducted a consumer product survey on the purchase of various models of personal computers. As part of that division, you are asked to write a program to analyze the data gathered in the survey. When you have finished writing your program, it should be tested with various data values, for example, the cases in which

- No models were purchased.

- Every model was purchased.

- No model was purchased by more than one consumer.

- Only one model was purchased, and it was purchased by many different consumers.

- Some models were purchased by many consumers, some by only one, and some by none at all.

By testing your program with a variety of data values, you can have greater confidence that it will produce the correct results when given arbitrary data.

79 Beat the bugs with instrumentation.

It has been said,

> Anyone who believes his or her program
> will run correctly the first time is either
> a fool, an optimist, or a novice programmer.

The best way to uncover logic errors in a program is to "get inside the computer," while your program is running and find out what values are actually stored there. This is not as difficult as you might think. You can include write statements in your program to trace the flow of control and

the values of the variables, or you can use an interactive "debugger," if such a facility is available on your system. The output of these debugging write statements or of a debugger is referred to as a trace; it is a listing of the values of the variables during execution of your code.

You will want to include debugging write statements at those points in your program where you believe an error might occur or where you are somewhat uncertain of your algorithm. These write statements should be included in the code when it is first written and should be left in for future debugging and maintenance. They may be included in an **if-then** statement and turned on and off with a boolean variable (a flag) or, alternatively, when the program fragment seems to be working properly, they may be commented out. It is best not to remove these statements because later you may find that the fragment still does not work correctly, and then you will have to go through the trouble of inserting them again. Furthermore, constantly entering and removing these write statements can, itself, introduce errors into your program.

When you first write your program, include the declaration of a variable, called, say, debugging. (You may even choose to declare several such variables.) Then, when you wish to debug a particular piece of code, you can set debugging to true. In the final version of the program, debugging can be set to false or, alternatively, its declaration might be changed from a variable to the constant false. Making debugging a constant is particularly a good idea if you have an optimizing compiler that eliminates code that is guarded by a condition that is constantly false. Then, the debugging code will still be present in the source program, but the object program will run without need for extra time or space.

Debugging write statements may be included as the first and last statements of each procedure and function to print the values of the parameters on entry and exit. For example,

```
procedure sort(var a: integerarray; numentries: index);
begin
  if debugging then
    begin
      writeln('Sort entered with the array a ordered ',
              'as follows: ');
      for i := 1 to numentries do
        write(a[i]:4);
      writeln
    end;
    .
    .
    .
  if debugging then
    begin
      writeln('Sort exited with the array a ordered ',
              'as follows: ');
      for i := 1 to numentries do
        write(a[i]:4);
      writeln
    end
end;
```

The portions of code that contain several levels of if-then-else statements are also excellent candidates for such instrumentation. Deep within these complicated blocks of code, there may be branches which the program should not take but might under certain erroneous conditions. Such branches should be identified and instrumented with debugging write statements.

For example, the local TV meteorologist, Atom Sphere, hired a programmer to write a program for use in making weather forecasts. In coding Atom's application, the programmer used the boolean variables raining and cloudy, which are set to true or false, depending on the weather conditions. In one part of the code, the programmer wrote

```
if raining then
   begin
      .

      .

      if cloudy then
         .

         .

      else
         writeln('Raining but not cloudy.    ',
                 'Error in procedure .. ');

      .

   end;  (* If raining block *)
```

Notice that the condition in which raining is true but cloudy is false could happen only under erroneous circumstances. The programmer planned for the possibility of such a condition by instrumenting the suspicious portion of code. If the programmer had omitted this simple instrumentation and such an erroneous condition had occurred, many hours might have been lost searching for the error and causing the computer to foul up the weather predictions.

Another place you may find it helpful to include debugging write statements is at the beginning of loops. However, be careful—if a loop is executed hundreds or thousands of times, you may be inundated with output! You might, therefore, choose to print the values of the variable only every tenth, hundredth, or thousandth time. For example,

```
while i <= 200 do
   begin
      if debugging and (i mod 10 = 0) then
         writeln('Entered while loop with i = ', i, ...);
```

   Alternatively, if you know that your program fails at a particular iteration of the loop, you may set the if statement to start printing when that iteration is reached.

   Debugging write statements may also be included around program blocks. This, alone, may not isolate the error. You may have to insert additional write statements to pinpoint the specific statement that is causing the error. For example,

```
if debugging then
    writeln('Before begin-end block identifiers = ', ...);
begin
    .
    .
if debugging then
    writeln('3 lines after begin, identifiers = ', ...);
    .
    .
if debugging then
    writeln('3 lines before end, identifiers = ', ...);
    .
    .
end;
if debugging then
    writeln('After begin-end block, identifiers = ', ...);
```

   Naturally, you will want to include identifying information, so that you know exactly where in your code the write statements occur that printed the results. These statements will help you to see intermediate results of the computation. Don't worry about the elegance of these write statements, but do print identifying information along with the results.

   Instead of using write statements to instrument your program for errors, you may choose to use a canned debugging aid, if such an aid is provided at your computer installation. Such an instrument, frequently called a debugger, is a computer program that allows you to interactively ask questions about the execution of your program in order to find logic errors or to test the code. Some debuggers even allow you to modify the code itself during execution.

Although each specific debugger will have its own commands, protocol, and capabilities, here is a list of capabilities that are available on some versions of this interactive debugging tool. You can

- Examine the values of any variables that may be of interest.

- Ask for information about how a particular variable was declared (integer, real, char, boolean, etc.)

- Find out how the program got to where it is; that is, you can list all of the procedures and functions that were called before the program reached its current point.

- Trace the execution of your program by printing (1) the value of an expression at a particular line of the code, (2) a message each time a particular source line is executed or a particular procedure or function is called, or (3) the value of a variable whenever it changes and the line at which it changes.

- Stop the execution of your program under specific conditions; for example, if a boolean variable becomes true or false, when (1) a specific line is about to be executed, (2) a procedure or function is about to be executed, or (3) the value of a specific variable is about to be changed.

- Modify your program code after you have temporarily stopped its execution.

- Continue the execution of your program after stopping it.

- Use the debugger as a calculator to check the values of mathematical expressions.

As you can see, a debugger is a powerful tool that can be a time saver during the debugging phase of programming. Consult your instructor or the consultants at your local computer center to learn whether there is a debugger available on your system. Then, request a copy of the user manual for the particular debugger. It's worth your time and effort to learn to use this tool properly.

80 A sleeping beauty needs attention.

Computers are fast! Don't be surprised if your program requires a ridiculously small amount of time to run. If, however, your program is doing nothing or appears to be doing nothing, it probably needs attention.

In particular, if your program takes more than a minute of processor time, chances are that it is caught in an infinite loop. Some interactive systems, particularly those at universities, have built-in time limits and will give you a message like

> Time limit exceeded

or, perhaps,

> Statement count limit exceeded

but other systems have no limit.

To eliminate infinite loops in your program, examine the `while` and `repeat` statements to see whether they terminate. If the boolean expression after the `while` never becomes false, or if the boolean expression after the until in a **repeat** loop never becomes true, then your program will be caught in an infinite loop. Remember, the loop must do something to change the truth or falsity of the condition in order to terminate. In loops that contain a compound condition, a common cause of nontermination is a mix-up between **and** and **or**.

For example, consider the following compound condition:

while (i >= 0) or (i <= 100) do

If i >= 0, then the condition is satisfied. If i < 0, then i <= 100 and the condition is still satisfied. Thus, the loop never terminates! To correct this problem, the **or** should be replaced by an **and**.

Goto's used sporadically throughout a program can also cause infinite loops. Many careless programmers have had code stuck in an infinite loop because of a series of **goto**'s that send the program into an unending sequence of jumps to different parts of their code. This is another of the many reasons why the **goto** statement should be avoided.

Infinite loops waste processor time, but time may also elapse without anything happening because your program is waiting for input at the keyboard. Don't forget to include prompts in your program, which ask the user to input data (as discussed in Proverbs 42 and 43); otherwise, your program may appear to be "hung" when it is actually just waiting for input from the user.

81 Off by one! Oh how dumb!

Off-by-one errors are errors that are caused because an action is done one time too often or one time too few. Off-by-one errors often do not generate error messages; they just generate wrong answers. To help prevent off-by-one errors, examine each program loop as soon as you write it. Examine the first and last cycles to determine how many times the loop is executed.

Here is an example of a program fragment that produces an error that is off by one:

```
(* Find the sum of the first n *)
(* positive integers.          *)
sum := 0;
num := 1;
while num < n do
   begin
      sum := sum + num;
      num := num + 1
   end;
```

This fragment actually finds the sum of the first n−1 positive integers because a < sign was used instead of a <=. Thus, the loop is executed one time too few. Convince yourself of this by hand checking the fragment.

Here is another program fragment that produces an off by one error.

```
(* Find the sum of the ten values *)
(* in the array value.            *)
i := 0;
total := 0;
repeat
   i := i + 1;
   total := total + value[i]
until i > 10;
```

In this case, after i has become equal to 10, the tenth value is added to total and the loop is entered again (once too many), causing either addition of the eleventh value in the array to total or a fatal run-time error if value is dimensioned to handle only 10 values. This error can be corrected by changing the > in the until line to = .

The for loop is usually less prone to off-by-one errors than the while or repeat loops. Thus, when you know how many times a loop is to be executed, you may prefer to use the for loop to avoid an off-by-one error. In any case, but particularly when you're using while and repeat loops, you should carefully hand check the loop to ensure that an off-by-one error does not occur.

82 Don't rebug when you debug.

Correcting your program once you have found an error requires some care. It is easy to introduce new errors while fixing old ones. Carefully evaluate the error and consider all the effects of making a change. Consider not only the test case that caused you to notice the error but, also, all the other cases for which the program must work. Do not change a program until you understand what it is trying to do and until you are confident that your change fits into that design. Never make a "quick fix" and hope for the best. Your quick fix is almost certain to come back and "bite" you later on.

With large programs it is necessary to be particularly careful when debugging. Nobody understands the whole of a large program, and it is likely that you will be debugging code that you did not design and, thus, do not understand very well. There have been many documented cases in which attempts to debug large programs have actually increased the number of errors in the programs.

When you have made a change to correct an error, repeat the entire test sequence. You already know that your change will make the current test work, because you designed it to do just that! But it is important to repeat all of the other tests to make sure that, while fixing this error, you did not accidentally introduce some other error.

Above all, don't rebug when you debug. The users of your program have probably found ways of living with bugs that they know about. It is unlikely that they will consider it an improvement if you replace these old familiar bugs with brand new ones.

83 Rewrite from scratch, rather than patch.

Occasionally, you may discover that during development, modification, or testing, the program on which you are working has become difficult to complete, hard to understand, or loaded with errors that are difficult to correct. Possibly, the requirements of the project have changed, and your program needs major revision to satisfy the new requirements. Or, perhaps you have inherited someone else's program that is written without regard to the structure and style that you would use.

When the code has been distorted by patching or written with a poor algorithm, it is best to start over. Go back to the **relax and think** stage and really start over. The time you have already put in working with the "bad" code will not have been wasted (you can use the experience for rewriting the program), and you will almost certainly save time in the future by avoiding a traumatic struggle with the old flawed code.

Don't let your ego get in the way. You will save time and come out with a stronger and better finished product if you reorganize and rewrite your program, rather than try to repair it from a poor foundation.

84 Behold your masterpiece.

When you've finished testing and debugging your program, sit back and behold the "masterpiece" you have created, and ask yourself the following questions.

- Does the program do what it was meant to do?

- Is the code well commented with meaningful comments?

- Is the code readable?

Be sure to check over your answers before leaving the computer lab with your "perfect" program. You might also ask someone, who is not familiar with the assignment but who is familiar with the language, to look at your program to see if it's as understandable as you thought.

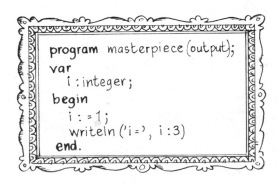

```
program masterpiece (output);
var
    i : integer;
begin
    i : = 1;
    writeln ('i =', i :3)
end.
```

Problems and Projects

1. Get a copy of the *ACM Computing Surveys* (Vol. 14, No. 2, June 1982), and read the article, "Validation, Verification, and Testing of Computer Software" by W. Richards Adrion, Martha A. Branstad, and John C. Cherniavsky, (pp. 159 to 192). Write a one- or two-page summary of this article.

2. The median of a collection of numbers stored in an array is the value that occurs in the middle of the array when it is sorted. If the number n of numbers in the array is even, then there is no exact middle, and the value just to the left of the middle is taken as the median. Write a function that takes an unsorted array of numbers, calls on a procedure to sort the numbers, finds the median, and returns this value. Write only a stub for the sort procedure. Use it to test that the median function works correctly. (Proverb 77 contains a discussion of stubs.)

3. Write a Pascal program that implements the interval bisection method for finding an approximate solution to an equation $f(x) = 0$. This method is described in the flowchart, data flow diagram, and pseudocode in Proverb 10. Test your program with values of a and b for which (a) $a = b$, (b) $a > b$, (c) $f(a) \times f(b) = 0$, (d) $f(a) \times f(b) > 0$, and for various functions f.

4. Examine the boundaries of the following fragment, which is intended to compute the mean, or average, of the numbers read in.

```
read (sentinel);
sum := 0.0;
k := 0;
repeat
   k := k + 1;
   read (a[k]);
   if a[k] <> sentinel then
      sum := sum + a[k]
until (a[k] = sentinel) or (k = 1000);
mean := sum/k;
```

What happens if 0 items are read in? If 1 item is read in? One student suggested the quick fix of dividing by k−1 instead of k. Is the program then correct? Rewrite the fragment as a while loop so that it is correct.

5. The following procedure is supposed to find the maximum element of an array containing n non-negative integers. Is it correct? If not, explain how you would go about debugging it systematically?

```
procedure findmax (var a: nonnegintarray;
                        n: nonnegint; var max: nonnegint);
var
   i: nonnegint;
begin
   max := 0;
   I := 1;
   while i < n do
      begin
         if max < age[i] then
            max := age[i];
         i := i + 1
      end
end;
```

6. Design and write the stub structure for a real estate sales management program. The program will use a file of records, one record for each home on the market, containing the address, number of bedrooms, number of baths, whether or not there is a garage, and price. The program should provide a menu of options so that a salesperson can request

(a) The information about a home located at a particular address.

(b) The information on all homes in a certain price range.

(c) The addresses of all homes for sale, with a particular number of bedrooms and baths, that are located in a particular city on a particular street.

7. Write a driver program for the merge and mergesort procedures given in Proverb 58. Include write statements in these procedures that will produce a trace of the values of the variables during execution of your program.

8. Write a nonrecursive version of the binary search function described in Proverb 56. Test your function for arrays of even and odd lengths and for different values of the key including

    (a) The smallest value in the array.

    (b) The largest value in the array.

    (c) A value smaller than the smallest value.

    (d) A value larger than the largest value.

    (e) A value not in the array but larger than the smallest value and smaller than the largest value.

    (f) The value in the middle position.

    (g) A value in the array but not in the middle.

    (h) A value that is duplicated.

9. Find out whether there is a debugger available on your system. If so, get a copy of the manual and read it. Then, write the program described below and use the debugger to debug it. When you are finished using the debugger, write a one-page report on the various features of the debugger that you used.

    The program will read words from a textfile and count the number of times each distinct word occurs. You may assume that each word contains, at most, 20 characters and that no words are split between lines. The program will print each distinct word and its associated count, starting with the word having the highest count and ending with the word having the lowest count.

10. Write a program to compute the interest, total amount due, and minimum payment for a revolving charge account. The program will accept the account balance from the last statement as input. A

finance charge of 2% of the unpaid balance will be added to the balance before any transactions are processed. Each transaction may be a purchase, refund, or payment. The minimum payment is 10% of the total amount due, provided that the amount is $10 or more; otherwise, it is the entire amount due. The program will print a statement for each customer, showing the account number, previous balance, finance charge, a list of transactions (kind and amount), and the final balance. The balances will be labeled with "credit" for an overpayment and "due" for a balance due. Include debugging write statements in your program to trace the values of the variables during its execution.

11. Complete the example in Proverb 77 for assigning letter grades. Write the details of the procedures and functions, testing each one as you complete it, using stubs for the remaining procedures and functions. As usual, the mean m is computed, using the formula

$$ m = \frac{\sum_1^n x_i}{n} $$

and the standard deviation σ is given by the formula

$$ \sigma = \sqrt{\frac{\sum_1^n (x_i - m)^2}{n}} $$

The letter grade will be determined by using the scheme of "grading on the curve." In this scheme, a letter grade is assigned to a numeric score x_i, as follows:

$$
\begin{array}{ccccccc}
m + \frac{3\sigma}{2} & < & x_i & \le & 100 & & A \\
m + \frac{\sigma}{2} & < & x_i & \le & m + \frac{3\sigma}{2} & & B \\
m - \frac{\sigma}{2} & < & x_i & \le & m + \frac{\sigma}{2} & & C \\
m - \frac{3\sigma}{2} & < & x_i & \le & m - \frac{\sigma}{2} & & D \\
0 & \le & x_i & \le & m - \frac{3\sigma}{2} & & F
\end{array}
$$

11
Documentation and Maintenance

For the grand finale, we present the proverbs for documentation and maintenance. A few of these proverbs may not seem to be of immediate relevance or importance to you as a student in programming classes; nevertheless, on the job you will find that using effective documentation and maintenance practices is essential for the survival of both you and your firm's software.

In this chapter you'll read about different kinds of documentation, depending on the target user, the estimated life of your program, and the level of its sophistication. You'll also read about practices for maintaining both your programs and their documentation. Just as the proverbs in preceding chapters become more meaningful to you when you put them into practice, so it is with the documentation and maintenance proverbs.

Now that you have learned some of the proverbs for writing successful Pascal programs, let's close by talking about how to document and maintain your successes!

85 Document!
Your program's life depends on it.

Some programmers view documentation as a task that they'd sooner avoid. After all, documentation means that they have to write in complete English sentences, using all of the rules of grammar that they learned in

school. Furthermore, it means that they have to take time away from the more glamorous activity of programming. Documentation does require some special skills besides those used in programming. However, it is an essential part of the software development process.

Effective documentation is important to everyone who is involved in producing, modifying, buying, or using programs. It is certainly important for firms that develop software for consumers. If the word gets around that an expensive software program has poor documentation, consumers may look elsewhere for their software needs. This is particularly true now that the software market has become so competitive.

Software teams that are casual about requiring effective documentation inevitably discover that modification of code is tremendously more difficult and expensive than it would have been if careful documentation standards had been followed. It's a case of "pay me now or pay me later." You can put some time into writing effective documentation during program development, or you can put in a lot of time when modifying your code, trying to figure out what you wrote months or years ago. Furthermore, because programmers are known to change jobs frequently, it makes sense for software managers to insist that program code is well documented. It's quite possible that the programmer may not be around in 6 months when the time comes for modifying the code.

Just as a software firm must be concerned with documentation, so must the programmer. As a student, you will probably be required to write your programs by yourself. You are the one-person software team, responsible for all aspects of software development, including documentation. However, in industry someone else may write the actual documentation for your programs. But you will still need to assist in the documentation process, so it is best if you understand effective documentation practices. Furthermore, if you enjoy technical writing, you may find a career in writing documentation both challenging and rewarding.

86 Automation needs a manual.

Once you have finished debugging your program, you will need to complete the documentation for it. You should have already produced the major sources of information for the documentation while developing and debugging your code: the structure charts, data flow diagrams, pseudocode, commented code, notes, working papers, and listings.

If you are the only person who will ever use your program, then you may not need to produce any written instructions on how to use or modify your code. In this case, the comments that you included in the code will suffice as documentation for your program. However, if other people will be using your program (this is very likely if you are being paid to write the program), there are two manuals, in particular, that should be developed as documentation for your code: the user manual and the technical manual.

The user manual, as the name implies, is the document that provides instructions on how to use a program. It should be written during the design phase of program development, before coding is begun. The reason for preparing this document so early in the software development process is that it can be an effective guide both for designing user-friendly programs and for planning the coding process.

The technical manual is designed to assist the maintenance programmers or software systems specialists in understanding and modifying a program. For very short programs, a listing of the program with low-level technical documentation may be adequate. Such documentation has already been discussed in earlier proverbs and includes descriptive comments, meaningful variable names, etc. But for large programs, especially for those with thousands of lines, a technical manual, which provides an overview of the high-level structure of your program, is a necessity.

Other manuals that might be needed include sales manuals to assist the marketing staff in developing strategies for marketing the software, field training manuals to help the sales personnel merchandise the software, and general information manuals to help consumers decide whether they should purchase the software.

87 Clear and correct is clearly correct.

It's likely that the end user of your program will not be interested in the inner workings of your program. The end user may simply be interested in running the program, providing some data to the program, and getting back the correct results. He or she may not even be familiar with computers or Pascal.

The user manual should, therefore, be written in nontechnical language and present an overview of what the program does. Most importantly, it should describe the input/output characteristics of the program for the user. It should include the following information.

- The program name.

- A concise description of what the program does, including an explanation of the results produced by the program and any assumptions that are made in the program.

- A brief (5-min) lesson on how to use the program, including a sample session that takes the user through each of the main steps.

- The sequence of commands needed to execute the program on the particular computer.

- The input data required by the program, including the order in which the data must be entered, the limits placed on the values, etc. If default values are used, they should also be indicated.

- The normal output produced by the program when it is given valid data. This should include an actual output listing of the program, with an explanation and interpretation of the computed values.

- The exception reports which consist of warnings, error messages, or abnormal output produced by the program when it encounters invalid data.

- Limitations of the program, such as limits on accuracy because of the physical characteristics of the particular computer, or limits on the amount of input because of fixed array declarations, etc.

- Customization notes on how to modify the program to fit a new configuration, if appropriate for the user.

- The name, address, and telephone number of the programmer, as well as the individual(s) responsible for providing assistance and maintenance.

The user manual should be written clearly and concisely and should provide the user with everything he or she needs to prepare the necessary data, run the program, and interpret the results. Remember that the quality of the documentation will influence the user's opinion of the software.

One computer company learned through experience the importance of clear and correct documentation when it introduced its new computer. The documentation was so confusing and full of errors that one customer decided to run an experiment on learning to use the computer with and without the documentation. Two equally experienced computer users were asked to learn to use the new machine. One was given the documentation, and the other was not given any. The person without the documentation learned to use the machine in a fraction of the time required by the other user. The user who was trying to learn to use the machine by reading the documentation was most likely confused by it and, therefore, was handicapped in the learning process. The computer company now puts much more effort into providing accurate and carefully tested documentation before it introduces a new machine.

88 Computers read Pascal; programmers need a technical manual.

A technical manual is an important reference for maintenance personnel and software engineers who need to know the inner workings of your code. Such a manual should describe the high-level structure of your program to aid them in understanding and modifying your code. The technical manual should include the following information.

- The program name.

- A description of what the program does, including an explanation of the results produced, the algorithms or methods used, and any assumptions made in the program.

- The historical development of the program, including the name, address, and telephone number of the programmer, as well as anyone responsible for program maintenance. It should include the date of the original version of the program, as well as descriptions and dates of changes, the testing of those changes, and acceptance of the changes.

- The overall program structure. This consists of a graphic diagram or a list of procedures and functions, together with their relationships to one another. This is where your structure chart and data flow diagram come in handy (see Proverb 10).

- A description of data structures, including name, type, and purpose, a list of the procedures and functions that access or modify the structure, the line numbers of the declaration, and initialization in the listing.

- A description of each procedure and function, including name, purpose, entry and exit conditions, the routines that call it, the routines it calls, the data items modified in it, and the line number in the listing.

- Maintenance aids, including notes on how to customize the program to fit a new configuration, instructions on how to use debugging or efficiency aids included in the program, etc.

Just as you targeted the user manual for its intended audience, be sure to write the technical manual so that it is targeted for the experienced technical personnel who will use it. If the technical manual is very brief, you might include part or all of it as comments in the code.

89 Test your documentation.

Before a company releases a new product, it conducts quality control tests on the product that it just produced. You too will want to maintain control over the quality of both your program and its documentation by testing them before they are distributed for use. One of the best ways of doing this is to give your program and its documentation to a friend or colleague to read over and use.

Although poor programs and documentation can be easy for you to overlook, they are usually quite evident to someone else. By having a friend or colleague read your work at various times during the development process, you can quickly eliminate unwarranted assumptions, unintentional omissions, unnecessary complexities, or just plain errors. Furthermore, you can check that your program and documentation are clearly written and understandable to someone else.

Ask a friend with little technical background to test the user manual, and ask a fellow programmer to test the technical manual. If they need motivation to read over your work, offer to buy them a drink if they will carefully edit your manuals. They may even feel flattered that you have chosen them as expert consultants to assist in improving the quality of your program and its documentation.

Of course, once you start the practice of quality testing among your colleagues, you will most likely be asked to read over someone else's documentation. When you do this, remember the proverbs, and be sure to point out any violations that you see.

Check the program for correctness by walking through it from the top down. First, check the main program and, then, the procedures and functions to see that they do what they were intended to do. Choose sample input, and calculate the output as if you were the computer. Finally, check the boundary conditions and other special cases to see that they are handled properly.

Use this same top-down approach in testing the documentation. Ask yourself: Are any major sections missing? Are there any glaring errors? Are any of the explanations confusing? After you have read the documentation, try running the program. Then discuss the program and its documentation with your colleague. You'll be doing him or her a favor by pointing out any flaws that you find.

90 Maintenance needs documentation, and documentation needs maintenance.

Many programmers spend a great deal of time modifying and maintaining code that was written by someone else. Nearly all programs are modified repeatedly over the life of their use, and most organizations spend much more time and money on maintenance than on new programs. Skilled maintenance programmers, and also programmers whose programs are easy to maintain, are highly valued.

Program maintenance consists of correcting, modifying, or updating a program due either to bugs in the program that were not originally discovered, to changes in the specifications of the program, or to changes in the equipment on which the program is run. If you were precise in your specifications, were careful to structure your program, and wrote clear, concise, and complete comments, then modification of your code should be relatively painless, and the maintenance programmers (a group that may very well include you) will be grateful that they do not have to reconstruct each step of the software development process or start over.

The proverbs to be followed in the maintenance phase of programming are similar to those followed in the testing and debugging phase. Remember the debugging write statements that you put in your program to trace the values of the variables and the flow of execution of your program? Don't remove them but leave them in as aids in maintenance, and turn them off and on with a switch (see Proverb 79). Of course, if the traces produced by these write statements are to be used by someone else, you will have to be more clear about printing identifying information along with the values of the variables.

As you become a more experienced programmer, you will want to think ahead about places in the code that may need to be changed in the future or that are potential bug "nests," so that in writing the program you can provide greater assistance in future code modification. Here are some further suggestions and recommendations for documentation and maintenance of your programs.

If an error exists, first document the error, including a statement of the symptoms of the problem and the conditions under which the error occurred. Then, determine what program corrections and changes are needed. Make sure that the proposed changes do not introduce new errors into other parts of your program. When you make a change in one part of your program, make sure that the change is consistent with other parts of your program that have not been changed.

Next, make the necessary corrections in a duplicate copy of the program. The original copy should not be altered until the changes in the duplicate have been checked out. The changes may result in such complete and utter disaster that your only recourse is to return to the original copy.

After you have made the required changes, you will need to test the program again. The program should be tested with the data that caused the failure to occur, as well as with the original test data. (For a discussion of testing, see Proverbs 75 to 84).

Once the corrected program has been checked out, the program, technical manual, and user manual must be updated to reflect the change that was made. A comment should be included in the program that gives the version, the date, and the name of the programmer who made the revision. The change should also be recorded in the technical manual, including

- A description of the error and the conditions under which it occurred, as well as its effects.

- The changes in descriptions, algorithms, diagrams, and the program itself in before-and-after formats.

- An update of the history, indicating the changes that have been made, together with their dates and line numbers.

If the input/output characteristics of the program have changed, then the user manual will also have to be updated. The changes should be brought to the attention of all users of the program, and copies of the revised program and its documentation should be made available to all persons who received the original program and its documentation. If you are thorough and consistent in your modifications, your work will be well accepted by your boss, fellow programmers, and end users.

Although software modification and maintenance may not seem very exciting to you initially, it is a very important skill that is worth mastering. Some people actually prefer this activity to software development; such people are in great demand. In professional environments, programs are modified, updated, and corrected all the time. Often, because of time and personnel limitations, modifications of limited importance cannot be made for years! Priorities are often attached to modification requests so that "hot" modifications, which need to be done as soon as possible, actually get done. Many full-time positions in software groups are not being filled because of the lack of competent professionals skilled in software modification and maintenance.

Problems and Projects

1. Much time is spent by programmers modifying existing programs to meet new specifications, rather than writing new programs from scratch. Modify the payroll program that you wrote in Chapter 4, Problem 6, so that it also computes and prints the

    (a) Number of employees processed.

    (b) Total hours worked.

(c) Total overtime hours worked.

(d) Total federal tax withheld.

(e) Total gross pay.

After you have made these modifications, consider how the documentation within your program aided you in making these modifications.
Was it adequate? How could it have been more helpful?

2. Proverbs 86 and 87 discuss preparation of the user manual for your
   software. Take a look at one of the user manuals at your local computer center, such as that for the Pascal compiler, operating system,
   or editor on your system. Look again at the list of recommended user
   manual contents in Proverb 87. Is the user manual missing anything
   on the list? Have you found something worthwhile in the user manual
   that is not on the list? Make a list of your findings. What is your
   opinion of the manual, and how would you improve it?

3. Write a user manual for the banking program in Chapter 6, Problem
   11. When writing the manual, assume that the users do not know
   Pascal and are naive about computers but do know how to log on and
   use a terminal.

4. Visit your local computer store and ask the salesperson which software packages have the best user documentation. Find out why some
   manuals are better than others and what it is that customers have
   difficulty with when using software and its documentation.

5. Write the user documentation for the automated grading program
   in Chapter 6, Problem 13, so that an instructor familiar with your
   computer, but unfamiliar with your program, could run it on the first
   try. Remember, clear and correct is clearly correct!

6. If possible, visit a local software firm or the computing department of
   a local firm. Find out what documentation standards are followed at
   the firm. Ask if you can look at some actual documentation. Compare the firm's documentation practices with those that the proverbs
   emphasize.

7. Write the code and technical documentation for a program of your choice. Exchange programs and documentation with a classmate and have him or her modify the program in some way. Discuss with him or her how useful your program and its documentation were in making the modification. How could the documentation have been more helpful? Could it have been more detailed and complete?

8. You have just been made lead project manager for Superfine Software Company. As an experienced programmer, you understand the importance of a complete documentation standard for your programming staff. Prepare a documentation standard for your staff of Pascal programmers. What manuals need to be written? How should comments appear in programs? What information should be included? Who is the target audience for each manual? Review the proverbs in this chapter to complete your standard.

9. Most programs in industry are written by teams of programmers. This assignment is intended to be done as a team project, in groups of three or four students. Each team will choose a documentation standard from those developed by its members in Problem 8 and will use this standard to write the code and documentation for a Pascal pretty printer.

   The program will read a Pascal program from one textfile and produce a pretty printed version of the program in a second textfile. Use the rules for indentation, spacing, and formatting that were suggested in Proverbs 26 and 27 and that were used in the examples in this text. To make the problem somewhat easier, assume that the conditional and iteration structures include statements delimited by **begin** and **end**. When you have finished writing the program and its documentation, discuss with the other members of your team how the documentation standard adopted by the team could be improved.

10. As a member of a team of three or four students, you are to write an interactive line-oriented text editor. This program will read text from an input file and write text to an output file, which is a copy

of the input file except for changes that result from commands issued by the user. Provide the user with a menu of options of commands, including

M *n*	Move ahead *n* lines from the current line.
T	Move to the top line of the file.
D *n*	Delete *n* consecutive lines, beginning with the current line.
I *text*	Insert the given text after the current line.
R *m n text*	Replace lines *m* through *n* with the given text.
C/*string1*/*string2*	Change the current line by replacing string1 with string2.
S *string*	Search the file, starting from the current line to find the next line that contains the string.
L *n*	List *n* consecutive lines, beginning with the current line.

After the project has been completed, write a paper that discusses the following points: How much time was spent by the group on each phase of the programming project? What difficulties did you experience in working with the group on the project? How would you do things differently the next time you're involved in a group programming project?

References

D. Cooper and M. Clancy, *Oh! Pascal!* (W. W. Norton, New York, 1982).

N. Dale and D. Orshalick, *Pascal* (D. C. Heath, Lexington, Massachusetts, 1983).

K. Jensen and N. Wirth, *Pascal User Manual and Report* (Springer-Verlag, New York, 1974).

IEEE, *American National Standard Pascal Computer Programming Language* (John Wiley & Sons, New York, 1983).

B. W. Kernighan and P. J. Plauger, *The Elements of Programming Style* (McGraw-Hill, New York, 1978).

H. F. Ledgard, J. F. Hueras, and P. A. Nagin, *Pascal with Style: Programming Proverbs* (Hayden Books, Rochelle Park, New Jersey, 1979).

G. M. Schneider and S. C. Bruell, *Advanced Programming and Problem Solving with Pascal* (John Wiley & Sons, New York, 1981).

G. M. Schneider, S. W. Weingart, and D. M. Perlman, *An Introduction to Programming and Problem Solving with Pascal* (John Wiley & Sons, New York, 1982).

Index

304   Index